PRINCE

MICK WALL

PRINCE

PURPLE REIGN

This edition first published in Great Britain in 2016 by
Orion
an imprint of the Orion Publishing Group Ltd
Carmelite House
50 Victoria Embankment
London EC4Y 0DZ
An Hachette UK Company

1 3 5 7 9 10 8 6 4 2

A CIP catalogue record for this book is available
from the British Library.

Hardback ISBN: 978 1 4091 6920 8
Trade Paperback ISBN: 978 1 4091 6921 5

Typeset by Input Data Services Ltd, Bridgwater, Somerset

Printed and bound by CPI Group (UK) Ltd, Croydon, CR0 4YY

The Orion Publishing Group's policy is to use papers that are natural,
renewable and recyclable and made from wood grown in sustainable forests. The
logging and manufacturing processes are expected to conform
to the environmental regulations of the country of origin.

Every effort has been made to fulfil requirements with regard to reproducing
copyright material. The author and publisher will be glad to rectify any omissions
at the earliest opportunity.

www.orionbooks.co.uk

For Linda Wall

Thank Yous & Acknowledgements

Heartfelt thanks to all those that helped make this book happen: Anna Valentine, Robert Kirby, Malcolm Edwards, Joel McIver, Chris Salewicz, Emma Smith, Jessica Purdue, Krystyna Kujawinska, Mark Handsley, Angela McMahon, James Macey, Mark Thomas, Vanessa Lampert, Steve Morant, Ian Clark and John Hawkins.

Contents

1

Purple Daze

Dispatcher: 911, where is your emergency?
Unidentified male: Hi there, um, what's the address here? Yeah, we need an ambulance right now.
D: Okay.
UM: We have someone who is unconscious.
D: Okay, what's the address?
UM: Um, we're at Prince's house.
D: Okay, does anybody know the address? Is there any mail around that you could look at?
UM: Yeah, yeah, okay, hold on.
D: Okay, your cell phone's not going to tell me where you're at, so I need you to find me an address.
UM: Yeah, we have um, yeah, we have um, so yeah, um, the person is dead here.
D: Okay, get me the address please.
UM: Okay, okay, I'm working on it.
D: Concentrate on that.
UM: And the people are just distraught.
D: I understand that they are distraught, but . . .
UM: I'm working on it, I'm working on it.
D: Okay, do we know how the person died?
UM: I don't know, I don't know.

D: *Okay.*

UM: *Um, so we're, we're in Minneapolis, Minnesota, and we are at the home of Prince.*

D: *You're in Minneapolis?*

UM: *Yeah, Minneapolis, Minnesota.*

D: *You're sure you are in Minneapolis?*

UM: *That's correct.*

D: *Okay, have you found an address yet?*

UM: *Yeah, um, I'm so sorry I need, I need the address here?*

Unidentified female: *7801*

UM: *7801.*

D: *7801 what?*

UM: *Paisley Park, we are at Paisley Park.*

D: *You're at Paisley Park, okay, that's in Chanhassen. Are you with the person who's . . .?*

UM: *Yes, it's Prince.*

D: *Okay.*

UM: *The person.*

D: *Okay, stay on the line with me.*

UM: *Okay.*

(Phone ringing)

Ambulance dispatcher: *Ambulance, Shirley.*

D: *Carver with the transfer for Paisley Park Studios, 78.*

AD: *Paisley Park Studios, okay.*

D: *7801 Audubon Road.*

AD: *Okay.*

D: *We have a person down, not breathing.*

AD: *Down, not breathing.*

D: *Yup.*

Purple is the most special of all the major colours, the one that appears the least frequently in nature. A synthesis of red and blue – male and female, fire and water, yin and yang – purple is always the colour that attracts the most attention.

In China, purple represents the harmony of the universe, spiritual awareness, a red purple symbolising fame and great fortune. In Japan, purple symbolises privilege and wealth – aristocracy. In Europe and America, for centuries the colour purple has been associated with vanity, extravagance and individualism, with magic and mystery. In parapsychology, people with purple auras are said to have a love of ritual and ceremony.

Now, since 1984, purple has become the colour symbolising the greatest musician of his generation, Prince, an artist for whom all of the above meanings would apply . . . 100 million records sold; seven Grammy awards; an Oscar; a multitude of BRITS, MTV and American Music Awards. A musical innovator on a par with David Bowie; a guitarist to rival Jimi Hendrix; a better dancer than James Brown; and a singer with more than one voice and many more ways than one of expressing it. Prince achieved more in his four-decade career than other artists achieve in a lifetime.

And then there were the women . . . A renowned lover of women who married and divorced twice, Prince was also linked with some of the most beautiful, glamorous and in many cases famous women on the planet, including Madonna, Kim Basinger, Carmen Electra, Nona Gaye (Marvin Gaye's daughter), *Twin Peaks* star Sherilyn Fenn, *Playboy* centrefold Devin DeVasquez, and almost all of the women he worked with professionally . . . Sheena Easton, Bangles singer Susanna Hoffs, former backing singer Vanity, Apollonia, who played Prince's love interest in the movie *Purple Rain*, Sheila E, another protégée. Even his two wives, Mayte Garcia, a former dancer, and Manuela Testolini, who worked for his charitable foundation, Love4OneAnother, were involved in Prince's work first.

His greatest love, though, as he was never shy of reminding us, was for God. He was born into a family of Seventh Day Adventists, and testifying was something he grew up doing, first in church, then later and for the rest of his life through his music. When, in later life, Prince became a Jehovah's Witness, it surprised everyone except those who'd known him since he was a boy. Prince could be playful, full of fun, but he took his God and his music – one and the same to him – very seriously.

All wrapped up in the most stunning and provocative fashions ever seen on *any* music star, Lady Gaga eat your heart out. Prince's look was as vari-focused as his music, raunchy yet androgynous; struttingly male yet teasingly feminine: silk, ruffles, pinks, lavish purples and red, topped off with beads, crucifixes, bippity-boppity hats, huge frilly cuffs and bared nipples – *thongs*!

Music, love, spirituality, sex, fame, God, clothes . . . This was the Prince his millions of fans around the world had come to know and love over the years. Yet at the time he died suddenly, tragically, on 21 April 2016, it seemed like the best of Prince's life and career was already over. His last worldwide hit single, 'The Most Beautiful Girl in the World', had been in 1994, his last multi-million selling album, a *Very Best Of* compilation from 2001.

Friends say he had money worries, personal issues, his last stage appearances – the 'Piano & a Microphone tour', in which he performed alone in mid-size theatres – a far cry from the days when he filled London's 20,000-capacity O2 arena for

21 nights, with a full-scale show that featured over a dozen different musicians, singers and dancers – weirdly truncated performances attended by the ghosts of his and his audience's shared, mixed-up, funked-out, purple pasts.

Then came the next day, as news of his passing rolled across the media landscapes of the world like a great tsunami of tears. First disbelief then shock, then grief, then wonder – then celebration and commemoration. In an era when social media gobbles up all the biggest stories and turns them into feather-light tweets, and a year when we have already seen so many celebrity deaths we have lost count (David Bowie, Terry Wogan, Victoria Wood, Harper Lee, Johan Cruyff, Alan Rickman, on and on . . .) news of Prince's death eclipsed them all. Not since the deaths of Elvis Presley and John Lennon has one star's passing had such a huge global impact.

This wasn't just the weeping and wailing of indiscriminate fandom, as with Michael Jackson, this was about a major cultural event. Prince's death didn't just make it into the tabloids, like the *Sun* and the *Mirror*, which both gave over their front pages to the news, but the great and the good of the media too; the *New Yorker* turning its front page purple; *The Times*, the *Telegraph*, and even the *Financial Times* putting the story on their front pages. TV news channels from CNN to Al Jazeera leading with the news; BBC TV documentaries hurriedly broadcast; endless highbrow obituaries bending the critical knee, the *Telegraph* putting it best when it explained imperially that Prince 'was to the pop music of the 1980s what David Bowie had been to that of the previous decade, its sole authentic genius'.

Then came the personal tributes . . . Elton John interrupting his show in Las Vegas to salute the 'Purple warrior', Boy

George tweeting 'I am crying!', Jimmy Fallon hosting a special Prince-themed edition of *Saturday Night Live*, even President Obama issuing a statement, which began: 'Michelle and I join millions of fans from around the world in mourning the sudden death of Prince.' Every major public space in Minneapolis – baseball and football fields, skyscrapers, churches and bars – was lit purple in remembrance. Whole cities across America bathed in the same beautiful but eerie commemorative purple light.

This wasn't just about somebody's music. Not just somebody's death. This was about all of our lives, whatever the colour. Lives lit purple. The one thing – after music, sex and God – Prince never tired of.

'He still loves royal purple,' Stacia Lang, Prince's former head of wardrobe at Paisley Park, once said. But also, 'red and chartreuse, and in brilliant colour combinations. Black and white too. He hates pea green, anything dull and muted. He gets bored very easily.'

We never got bored of Prince, though. Even when we began losing count of the recordings he was releasing – 39 albums in 37 years with enough unreleased material still in the vault to release a new album every year for the next 100 years – we never grew tired of the stories about him. Did he *really* sleep with Boy George, as the former Culture Club singer half jokingly claimed on *The Voice*? (No.) Did he *really* put on the best halftime show in Superbowl history? (Yes.) Did he *really* do all the outlandish things he said and did? (Yes and no. But mainly yes!)

Did he ever really know, though, how deeply loved he was by his fans, by his followers, by the people that just adored the very idea of him?

The answer to that last remains doubtful. Prince, for all his shocking bravado, was also a deeply insecure person. As one former friend commented in the days after his death, 'It's like he was afraid of the fame but then when it was gone he'd miss it and crave it.'

One minute up, the next minute down. It was this basic humanity, this perceived frailty, that lay at the heart of his popularity. Prince didn't parade his victories like modern rappers; he hid behind masks, retreated from the press. The beautiful women in Prince's stage show and videos were not treated like hos, but as goddesses. Could anyone but Prince have written something as genuinely soulful and touching as 'If I Was Your Girlfriend'?

At a time when Michael Jackson was busy proclaiming himself to be the King of Pop, Prince smiled that secret smile and said: 'I don't want to be king of anything. My name is Prince and I'm a normal person.'

Then he abandoned his own name and insisted he simply become known by a symbol – the 'love symbol' as it became known. Inspired by a lengthy contract dispute with his record label, even after Prince was freed from his contract with Warner Bros. he incorporated the symbol into his iconography: microphones in the same shape, even his purple guitar.

That's why when we heard of his death none of us could quite believe it. Prince? But he wasn't like all the drinkers and drug takers in the entertainment world, he wasn't like the others, he was from another realm, surely Prince would live for ever?

Let's go back to the 'love symbol'. What the critics – huffing and puffing about having to find a new font to include the symbol in their copy, indignant that someone would turn his nose up at what was reportedly a $100 million contract – missed when they pushed themselves to explain the glyph with it's 'astrological symbols for male and female in a form that resembled a sceptre', was its true significance.

Prince's so-called 'love symbol' was in reality a pop representation of the Ankh, or the Crux Ansata – two interlaced triangles making a circle surmounting the Tau Cross (the type of cross which follows the shape of the letter 'T'). The Ankh is an Egyptian symbol of great antiquity and it portrays the resurrection of the spirit out of its encasement of matter, otherwise expressed as the triumph of life over death, of spirit over matter, of good over evil. The message of love Prince was sending then, long before his death, was that of eternity, or heaven, of a life beyond death.

And you can hear that message in every significant musical work he created.

As Prince sang on one of his best-known hits, 'Let's Go Crazy', life was the 'electric word' and it meant for ever. 'But I'm here to tell you there's something else,' he sang in the same song, 'The afterworld . . .'

That's where he is now. And that's where we can still know him. Through his music, and our memories of him.

Unlike Bruce Springsteen, Madonna, Michael Jackson — the other giants of eighties music – Prince was the only one that never relied on producers and regular co-writers to help conceive his art. As soon as he became famous he didn't flee his home and make a run for New York or LA. He stayed where he was and built his palace of dreams – Paisley Park – where he could still breathe the same air he'd grown up on. A boy from the Midwest city of Minneapolis who never lost his Midwestern family values, staying home, away from the flash-and-grab of Hollywood or Manhattan, in a place where everyone respected him, idolised him – and gave him the privacy and space he needed.

There were no rules for Prince, no maps for him to follow drawn by other people. Just the steps up that ladder he so famously preached about, that he chose for himself. He was, as the American writer Bob Lefsetz pointed out in the days following Prince's death, 'about the power of music. Especially when made by someone who seemed beholden to the sound as opposed to the adulation, to the music as opposed to the money, to the song as opposed to the stardom.'

And that's what this book is about. The life, yes, the death, of course, but mainly that 'something else' Prince sang about and believed in – and which he helped us to believe in, perhaps even more now he's gone.

Sleep tight, sweet Prince . . .

2
Little Man, Big Dreams

Dig if you will the picture . . .

It is 1970. Prince is 12 years old. At 5 feet 2 inches he's already stopped growing. As if to compensate he's allowed his dark hair to grow into what his friend, Jimmy Harris, later describes as 'the biggest afro in the world'.

He doesn't talk much. Doesn't yet fill rooms with his presence. But boy does he know how to play . . . Piano, guitar, drums, bass, trumpet, saxophone, you name it, this kid knows how to play it. Today it's guitar. He's on stage at a talent show at his high school, Bryant Junior. Jimmy's on drums and he can't believe what he's hearing from the little kid with the big guitar.

'At twelve years old he knew note for note the whole solo in "Make Me Smile" by the group Chicago,' he recalled in 1992, 'and that was a really intricate solo. I was just *blown away*!' So blown away he was still telling the story in the days that followed Prince's death 45 years later. 'He was brilliant even at that age.'

Afterwards, everyone was asking: *Who was that kid?*

It's a question we're still asking today. The answer something even Prince was still struggling with at the time of his death. The story too strange, too painful, too tragic, even when times were at their most wonderful, just *too damn much*, for him to ever come fully to terms with. Let alone a world constantly judging him, saying so much and revealing so little, getting all the tiny details so wrong so often he gave up doing interviews for over 20 years, wearied and disgusted at the very idea that anyone could ever really know him when he felt he barely knew himself for much of that time. To the point where he even gave up his own name. And still they wouldn't leave him alone, wouldn't even try to understand.

The facts were simple but the truth was always so much more complicated. Born at Mount Sinai hospital, in Minneapolis, on Saturday, 7 June 1958. A Gemini. Before you say you don't believe in astrology, consider this: characteristically, Geminis are extremely independent. They will not be pinned down by anyone or any rules. They need to experience the world on their own. Change and freedom are extremely important to Geminis, they will never let anyone dictate to them, and freedom is essential to their mental well-being. Sound like anyone you know?

'All I Have to Do is Dream' by the Everly Brothers was the number one single in America at the time, an omen perhaps for the boy who would spend his entire life working on how to make his most extravagant dreams come true. (More amusingly, the record that followed it to the top spot just two weeks later was 'The Purple People Eater' by Sheb Wooley, with its some might say prophetic refrain of: *'Well bless my soul, rock and roll . . . Pigeon-toed, undergrowed, flyin' purple people eater . . .'*)

He was named Prince Rogers by his father, John Nelson, a workman and part-time musician, who dreamed of his son 'doing everything I wanted to'. John was a gifted jazz pianist who had once fronted his own jazz Big Band, but now settled for occasional gigs around town leading The Prince Rogers Trio. John, a quiet, sometimes stern man, frustrated at seeing his life taken over by the responsibilities of raising a large family, and his wife, Mattie Della Shaw, a talented former singer in the style of Billie Holiday, were already struggling to feed a family of four when Prince was born.

Growing up in a small home on Logan Avenue in North Minneapolis, times were hard. North Minneapolis held the highest concentration of violent crimes of the Twin Cities – the joint name given to Minneapolis and sister city St Paul – and what John earned from his job at the local Honeywell plant (an industrial supplier) barely covered the basics. His occasional gigs around town with his trio helped supplement that income, but Mattie – who Prince later described as having a 'wild side' – began to feel trapped. Two years later their youngest child, their daughter, Tyka Evene, would be born, and things got even harder.

Mattie took to calling her youngest son Skipper. Whether, as often later said, it was simply to distinguish him from his father, who liked to be known by his stage name, or because she wanted to divert her son away from following in his father's footsteps, Prince's path was set from the moment, aged five, he first saw his father play at a small local theatre. At first Prince Senior appeared to be playing alone at the piano but then the curtains parted and suddenly out bopped a line of barely clad dancing girls. People in the audience began to stamp and cheer. 'From then on I think I wanted to be a musician,' he later claimed.

John would encourage Prince to learn on his piano, his sister Tyka singing along, as John and Mattie had done together in a previous life. Other times, he would chase Prince away, appalled at the way his young son banged away at the keys. But the boy was not discouraged. He picked up any instrument that came within his grasp. Accompanying his mother on expeditions to local department stores, he would go and sit at pianos, organs, and play while Mattie did the shopping. One day Prince came into the piano room sheepishly and showed his father a strident little melody he had written, which he called 'Funk Machine'.

It wasn't just his father's musicality the boy took note of though. John still harboured dreams of stardom. In contrast to all the available evidence – he was no longer young and the spots around town where a jobbing musician could earn good money were predominantly the territory of white musicians – John would often walk around the house dressed as if to go onstage, and drove a sleek Thunderbird convertible, a legend in his own mind, at least part of the time. Years later, Prince would do the same. Never knowingly underdressing and wearing stack heels even at home, though by then he had invented a more prosaic reason for always staying in character, no matter where he was. When he was 20, he recalled, 'I had some old clothes on because I was going to help a friend move house and some girls came by and one went: "Oh my god, Prince!" And the other girl went' – pulling a face – '"That ain't Prince." I didn't come out of the house raggedy after that.'

Mainly Prince's childhood can be characterized as one of overcompensating for life's challenges. He was epileptic until he was seven, his seizures triggered by seemingly anything: low blood sugar, high blood pressure, fevers and headaches, bad reactions to food or medicines – or none of those things. It meant everyone around him – his parents, teachers, siblings – had to be constantly vigilant. Until one day, he recalled, he told his mother: '"Mom, I'm not going to be sick any more," and she said, "Why?" and I said, "Because an angel told me so."' He never had another epileptic fit.

A lonely child who found it hard to socialize, years later in a famous TV interview with Oprah Winfrey, he talked of being in therapy and experiencing a 'total recall' of his early childhood, discovering a second person inside himself; an invisible friend he'd made up when he was five. 'You know,' he said coyly, 'somebody to care about you and love you and be your friend and not ridicule you.' He paused, smiled that secretive little smile he was always so good at and added, 'We haven't determined what sex that other person is yet . . .'

Growing up in a predominantly white city, the youngest son of two mixed-race parents, at a time when the Civil Rights movement in America was gathering huge momentum, he couldn't help be 'conscious', he said, of his ethnicity, even as he insisted later on that colour was never an issue for him. 'The first time I saw a person of colour in a book,' he recalled, 'the person was hung from a tree. That was my introduction to African-American history in this country . . . I know that experience set a fire in me to be free.'

He was just nine when he discovered one of the other great defining passions of his life and work: sex. He'd sift furtively through his mother's substantial collection of porn magazines that she kept hidden in her bedroom. 'She had a lot of interesting stuff. Certainly that affected my attitude towards my sexuality.'

In real life, other kids in the school playground could be cruel. Shorter than other children his age, he was teased and called 'Princess'. With his striking visage – the result of a mixed-race lineage because his father was a light-skinned

African American while his mother was a mix of African American, Native American and white Italian – he was pilloried and called 'Butcher's Dog'.

He responded to such vile taunts by willing himself to be good at everything he did – including, amazingly, basketball. Playing in the point guard position – the equivalent of a midfield general in football – according to Jimmy Harris Prince 'could distribute, had great handles, and could shoot the lights out . . . He was short but he had confidence.' And speed. As he ran up and down the court like a streak of lightning, girls would scream and call his name. That was another thrill – like music – he would fast become addicted to.

That hard-won confidence suffered a terrible blow though in 1968, when his parents, whose family rows had now escalated out of control, finally separated. John moved out. Prince was devastated, but even more shocked by the fact his father left behind his precious piano. Prince would console himself by sitting at the piano playing, but Mattie disapproved. For Mattie, her husband's frustration at not making it as a musician was what had finally driven them apart. She was damned if she was going to allow Prince to fall into the same trap. Instead, she doubled down on the boy, discouraging his obsession with music, sending him to an array of different, mainly white schools, in the hope he would turn out to be someone with a job she could really be proud of.

In a breakthough interview with Andy Schwartz, of the highly influential American magazine *New York Rocker*, in June 1981, Prince said: 'I think music is what broke [my mother] and my father up, and I don't think she wanted that for me,' Prince explained in one of his first interviews. 'Musicians, depending on how serious they are, they're really moody. Sometimes they need a lot of space, they want everything just right sometimes, you know. My father was a great deal like that . . .'

Prince would hide his socks in the vain hope that his mother would allow him to stay off school that day, but Mattie would always find a new pair and force him out the door. Prince put up with it, even as his passion for playing music grew ever stronger. But when his mother met and married another man, Heyward Baker, the situation reached breaking point.

Baker tried to involve himself in his new stepson's life. When he took Prince to a James Brown concert, he arrived home that night and immediately started imitating the singer's classic stage moves. But Baker could also be taciturn, sensed Mattie disapproved of her son's very obvious fascination with music and reportedly only spoke up when telling Prince off for doing something wrong. 'I disliked him immediately,' Prince would later insist. That may or may not have been true. But as he told Chris Salewicz in an early interview, 'It's very difficult having a stepfather – basic resentment all the way around. Nobody belongs to anybody.'

Prince was 12 when he decided to run away. Though not very far, turning up at the door of the small apartment in downtown Minneapolis his father had moved into when he left home. Father and son lived together for just a few months. John was still working at the plant by day and playing piano by night, the musical accompaniment in a series of strip clubs and clip joints. The two hardly spoke, though Prince was expected to fully abide by his father's rules. That was all right while Prince remained devoted to music and basketball. But he was also now discovering girls. Or rather, girls were discovering him.

He was 14, claimed to have lost his virginity long before, and took to inviting girlfriends back to his place when his father was out, which was most nights. But when John came home one night and found his son in bed with a girl, he went crazy and threw them both out on the street, telling Prince not to bother coming back. Prince spent the next two hours crying in a phone booth, calling his father and begging to be allowed back in, only to have his father hang up on him. In desperation he pitched up at his Aunt Olivia's house. Olivia was as strict as John. Worse, she didn't own a piano. Prince kept calling his father and over the days and weeks John allowed his son back into his life – but only on certain weekends. Taking pity on him for being unable to play piano any more, John bought his son a cheap electric guitar, and looked on amazed as the boy taught himself to play it virtually overnight.

It was now that Prince moved towards forming his own band. An old boyhood friend from church, Andre Simon Anderson (André Cymone), suddenly came back into his life after his parents split and his mother, Bernadette, was forced to move herself and her six kids into a house in North Minneapolis. Prince and André were the same age, enjoyed the same kind of interests – music and girls – and the two became fast friends. There was another connection: André's father, Fred, had once been the bass player in John Nelson's band. André had picked up the habit and taught himself bass.

Along with Prince's cousin Charles on drums, the three teenagers began playing together at Aunt Olivia's. Soon they were joined by André's sister, Linda, on keyboards, and a couple of high school pals named Terry Jackson and William Doughty on various percussion instruments. They named themselves Phoenix after the 1972 album of the same name by proto-heavy metallists Grand Funk Railroad, whose hit single that year, 'Rock & Roll Soul', was a big favourite of Prince's.

But it wasn't just the chunky gospel organ and high-fiving guitars they admired; they also took to playing 'I Want You Back' by the Jackson 5, with Prince doing a can't-tell-the-difference imitation of 14-year-old Michael's high-pitched lead vocals.

By the time they actually started playing small concerts – under their new name, Soul Explosion – mainly talent shows and high-school dances, their repertoire had expanded to include material from Stevie Wonder, Jimi Hendrix, Grover Washington and Sly & The Family Stone, and a host of classics by major rock artists like Joni Mitchell, Carole King, even Led Zeppelin and Fleetwood Mac. For Prince, growing up switching on the radio between local black station KUXL and white rock station KQRS, music held no colour barrier. Eventually, though, even that proved too formulaic for him. 'Listening to the radio there really turned me off a lot of things that were supposedly going on. If they did pick up on something they'd just play it to death, and you'd end up totally disliking it. So I missed out on a lot of groups.' There was only good and bad stuff. Prince was inspired by the good stuff whatever the colour of the skin of the people bringing it.

Finally, Aunt Olivia couldn't stand the noise any more and told her nephew he'd have to leave – immediately. This time it was André's mother, Bernadette, who took pity on Prince, allowing him to move into the basement of their house on Russell Street.

Twenty years later, Prince would release a song called 'The Sacrifice of Victor', on which he thanked 'Bernadette a lady', who taught him, he sang, of the virtues of 'discipline' and 'sacrifice'. Owen Husney, his first manager, whom he met in 1976, recalled visiting Prince and finding the basement flooded. Prince shrugged it off, telling him it was always flooded in winter – and why he'd built stilts for his bed, which he would hop onto with his guitar via some raised wooden planks he had nailed together.

Linster 'Pepé' Willie, a slightly older musician, from Brooklyn, who met him through his girlfriend and later wife, Prince's cousin Shauntel, remembers being collared by the 15-year-old, who would question him for hours about the labyrinthine machinations of the music business: the numerous ways musicians could lose money and even control their own music; and, most important, the only ways musicians could ensure they *didn't* get ripped off. The most important lesson Pepé taught Prince was about song publishing, later helping him to set up his own publishing company, Ecnirp (Prince spelled backwards). So that when the major record labels did finally come calling, Prince was in a position to refuse to grant them any publishing rights – standard practice in record contracts back then and the main reason Prince's is now one of the world's most valuable.

Pepé ended up enlisting Prince in recording sessions for his own band, 94 East, named after the freeway corridor that connects Minneapolis to St Paul. Prince would appear intermittently on various demos until his solo career took off, writing one number for them, 'Just Another Sucker', which prefigured his own later sound in the early Eighties.

Prince's original compositions for his own band, meanwhile, were now taking unexpected new directions. Fading fast were the boxy little funk jams, to be replaced by a whole raft of six- and seven-minute epics that combined sci-fi, sexual fantasy and low-rider melodrama that occasioned another name change – to Grand Central. When Charles began missing rehearsals, they made another change, bringing in a shy, quietly spoken friend of André's named Morris Day to play drums. Charles considered the move cold and calculating.

As New Power Generation's future drummer Michael B would point out to the writer Phil Sutcliffe in 1992, 'You see, he's been Prince a *long* time!' He had to be. The local Minneapolis scene was small but highly combative, because of the harsh Minneapolis winters, where it would snow for three solid months.

'We would be indoors all through the winter practising a lot,' recalled rapper-dancer Tony M, 'sharing whatever equipment we had. Then in the summer, all the bands were battling each other for the same gigs. It was very competitive.'

Indeed, Minneapolis's black north side was home to a number of promising young outfits in the mid-Seventies. As well as Prince's Grand Central, there were Family, whose Pierre Lewis was leading the way with the latest synthesisers, Cohesion, whose drummer, Rocky Garretty, would later find success with Alexander O'Neal, and Prophets of Peace, who specialised in horn-heavy funk. And, most threatening of all, Flyte Tyme, which featured the future star production duo Jimmy Jam and Terry Lewis, and future solo singer Alexander O'Neal. Teenage Prince took careful note of them all. It was Sonny Thompson, of Family, that most people from those days credit as being the guy who really showed Prince how to play bass. 'He'd be down in the basement there, smoking a cigarette, playing bass with the wah-wah,' Michael B told Sutcliffe, 'and Prince would just sit and watch him for hours': something Prince never forgot, going back and recruiting Thompson, now billed as Sonny T, for his Nineties band, beginning with the *Diamonds and Pearls* album. 'We all dreamed as kids,' Thompson said of those early days in the basement with Prince. 'But he did it.'

It was also around now that Grand Central decided to tweak their image, sporting smooth-looking suede jackets with their zodiac signs on the back – taking on a much more professional approach to their stagecraft, inspired by their new manager, Morris's mother, Lavonna Daugherty. Prince now had a band that felt like family, his life directed by two older, strong women: Lavonna and Bernadette.

Still, he was frustrated at the lack of money, terrified he would end up like his father, only a part-time musician. He hated school, which he only stayed at because Bernadette absolutely insisted, and began to earn a reputation for being overly provocative. 'I didn't really notice Prince till he walked through the schoolyard one day wearing just an open trench coat and a pair of underpants,' remembered Damon Dickson, who years later would form part of the New Power Generation's dazzling dance team. 'We just looked and said, what the hell is *that*?'

He would now fight anybody who dared make fun of his height or his name. 'People would say something about our clothes or the way we looked or who we were with, and we'd end up fighting,' he later recalled. 'I don't know if I fight fair, but I go for it.' And he took to hanging round the local McDonald's sniffing the air wishing he had enough money for one of their giant cheeseburgers. If it wasn't for his precocity at music, the few friends he had might have abandoned him too.

He was 17 when Lavonna paid for the band to go into a professional local studio and record a six-track demo. Months later, when the demo still hadn't led to a record deal, he took to writing a succession of more commercial songs, a dozen new songs a week, forcing the band to take on additional musicians and change their name yet again, this time to Shampagne – a 12-piece band with half of them only pretending to play instruments. It was the spectacle Prince was seeking. Something that matched his ever more ambitious musical ideas.

Another session was booked, at an eight-track studio called Moon-Sound, named after its owner, Chris Moon, a 24-year-old white Englishman with an afro. When Moon called Prince that night and asked if he'd like to put some piano on a few acoustic tracks of his own – and said that, crucially, he would pay for his time – it was the beginning of a new musical relationship. At the subsequent session, Prince ended up playing piano, bass and drums, before adding sumptuous layers of backing vocals.

Blown away, Moon suggested they hook up and work together full-time. He couldn't afford to pay him. Instead he offered Prince his own key to the studio and gave him lessons on how to work the equipment. Suddenly self-sufficient, Prince began virtually living at the studio. 'He'd stay the weekend, sleep on the studio floor,' said Moon. Suddenly, Prince didn't need Shampagne any longer. He quit the next day. Shampagne, he complained, 'was all Top 40 stuff. The audiences didn't want to know the songs I was writing for the group. They'd just cover their faces largely because of the lyrics. I remember I had this song called "Machine" that was about this girl that reminded me of a machine. It was very explicit about her, uh, parts. People seemed to find it very hard to take.'

But if Prince had felt frustrated at trying to build a career around a band, working alone with Chris Moon proved even more stressful. Moon knew all about studios but he only played an acoustic guitar. Prince could now work the studio and play any instrument you put in front of him. He began to resent Moon's insistence on directing their sessions together. Within six months Prince was writing, playing, singing and producing his own sessions. Moon still pitched in with notes but Prince simply ignored him.

When they had enough tracks recorded for an album, Prince set out – alone – for New York. Staying at his older half-sister Sharon's place in nearby New Jersey, he spent a few weeks trying to get someone to listen to his tapes. 'I think I didn't get the "big deal" when I first came to New York,' he told the writer Andy Schwartz, 'I was writing things that a cat with ten albums would have out, like seven-minute laments that were, you know, gone. I wrote like I was rich, like I had been everywhere and seen everything and been with every woman in the world.'

Still no dice. New York was the centre of the American music business. But you couldn't get through the doors unless you had recognised professional representation. Prince returned to Minneapolis a chastened figure. Then Moon had another idea: a contact he'd made named Owen Husney.

Husney was a 27-year-old marketing whiz who had once played guitar in a Minneapolis garage-rock band named The High Spirits, who'd enjoyed a minor hit in the mid-Sixties with a revved-up version of Bobby 'Blue' Bland's '(Turn On Your) Love Light'. When he listened to the cassette Moon brought him he was intrigued by the material: some of the tracks were up to 12 minutes long. This was clearly a gifted outfit. When the last track ended he asked Moon to tell him about the group.

Moon just looked at him and said: 'It's one seven-teen-year-old kid.'

Moon now had Husney's full attention. The material was experimental, but catchy; long but musically inventive. But none of that impressed as much as the fact that it was made by *one 17-year-old kid.*

Moon had to be shitting him, surely? No, insisted Chris. Husney jumped. 'Get him on the phone now.' What was his name?

'Prince.'

When they spoke on the phone, at first Prince was suspicious. This guy was too much, telling him how great he was, that he should produce his own records, that he should come and see him a.s.a.p., get some kind of deal going. By now he'd also been getting phone calls from some cat in LA, also talking to him about handling his career, talking record deals and management. Overwhelmed, unsure how to handle the sudden attention, Prince went back to his basement and talked it over with André, who couldn't understand what his friend was waiting for.

Eventually, Prince met Husney, got on with him immediately, and, in December 1976, agreed to sign to his new manager's own hastily formed production company, American Artists Inc. Husney had managed to raise $50,000 to start the company, but he only had one artist on it – Prince, whom he now relocated to his own downtown apartment. He also furnished him with brand new instruments, some regular monthly spending money and a whole new sense of direction and purpose. Not least, the repeated insistence – a stroke of genius, in retrospect – that when they came to record, Prince should produce himself, Husney rightly reasoning that no outsider would have the same individualism that Prince showed in his recordings.

Though he was just 18 and still not entirely sure about the big idea of producing his own records, one thing Prince could not argue with was Husney's total commitment. 'Owen believed in me,' Prince shrugged. 'He really did.' Husney, he recalled, would impress upon him that 'when he was coming up, people were trying to do something different from the next cat. I guess that's probably how psychedelic music came into being, because everybody was trying to be so out and crazy, it just went overboard. But I think that's the way to be.'

All Prince had to do now, said Owen, was come up with the goods. So it was that early in 1977 Prince was booked into Sound 80 Studios to record a new, much more professional demo, with three tracks, 'Soft and Wet', a long trippy, deliciously naughty version of one of the original Moon co-writes; 'Make It Through the Storm', a breezy pop-soul confection; and 'Baby', another sweet soul number that betrays Prince's love of the sugared vocal harmonies of The Stylistics.

Still almost cripplingly shy about performing on his own in the studio, but fully in command of his vocals and playing, he wowed the engineer, David Rivkin, by singing all the instrumental parts into a small cassette recorder, as a guide for each track. Then insisting on the studio lights being turned off while he sang.

Husney was also deeply impressed by Prince's determination not to get involved in the drinking and drugging that so often characterise a young musician's life. After a session was over, he never hung out and got high with the guys. Instead he went straight to sleep on the floor of the studio, or sat up talking to Husney about his dream to take his music to Number 1 in the charts. Not just that but to be a movie star too. And eventually to produce other artists.

Husney would chuckle to himself as he drove home each night. The kid had big dreams. But that was cool. At that age you were allowed to have the kinds of dreams that would almost certainly never come true.

According to the young Prince, he would 'play-act my whole future. I willed this whole trip . . . It's almost a curse.'

3

Wanna Be

These days we look back at the life and career of Prince and we see his worldwide success as obvious, almost fated. He could play everything, he could sing anything, he could dance, write, produce and have sex on stage with his guitar and still retain an air of mystery. Of course he became a star! What else could he possibly have been?

In reality, it took a lot more than just his raw talent, however prodigious, to get Prince noticed by the major players of the American music biz in the late 1970s. It took hustle. And plenty of it. Fortunately, in Owen Husney, Prince had exactly the right man for the job. Husney wasn't just experienced and well-funded, he had street smarts. His first job was to put together a promotional package for his new artist. Not just something shiny and professional, the record labels were inundated with those, but something that was truly eye-catching. Something you didn't see every day.

First off, he put Prince together with a young New York photographer named Robert Whitman. Whitman wasn't your run-of-the-mill rock photographer or even celebrity-baiter, he saw himself as an artist in his own right and he spent several days working with Prince, trying to capture a defining image of him. There were the standard headshots, with Prince's afro made to stand out even more by use of special lighting; semi-casual shots of the young artist at the piano and sitting around with a guitar cradled in his arms. Shots of Prince strutting down the street flipping Robert the bird. Shots of Prince with his shirt off; shots from behind, emphasizing his tight ass. Shots of Prince with a big cheesy grin.

With the pics in the bag, Whitman turned his attention to the rest of the promotional material. But rather than include a lengthy biography, copies of press notices and the usual bumph that goes into these things – and which invariably end up in the record exec's wastepaper basket – Whitman hit on the idea of including pieces of paper with just one sentence on them. The idea was to bait the hook just right, make any prospective viewer want to know more. They also trimmed two years from Prince's real age, making him just 17. The finishing touch was when they also sent out Prince's demo on reel-to-reel tapes, unheard of since the days before cassettes came in, but a sure signifier that this kid, Prince, was not like the others.

Eventually 15 promo kits with tapes were made, of which half went out, one at a time, to every major record label in America. When two weeks later Husney had received not one response, he took matters a step further. He phoned Warner Bros. and told them too bad, but his wonder kid client was now being courted by CBS, who wanted to fly him out to LA to sign him. Husney might be able to get someone from Warner's in for a quick meet if they wanted but they'd have to hurry. A Warner exec, Russ Thyret, said yes, count me in. Then Husney rang CBS and A&M to tell them Warner had stepped in quickly to sign Prince up, and that they were flying him out to LA so if they were interested they had better move fast. Again, both labels jumped at the chance to get their feet in the door before Warner's. Then Husney repeated the trick with RSO and ABC Dunhill. 'Record companies always want to go straight to where lightning has already struck,' explains Atlantic Records' former president Phil Carson.

There was still one last ace up Husney's sleeve. Out on the West Coast in the late Seventies, record execs still showed up for work in faded blue jeans, T-shirts with band logos and shiny tour jackets. It was all about the vibe, man. Many still sported silver coke spoons dangling from their necks. So Husney insisted that when he, and Prince, and their attorney, Gary Levenson, flew down to LA, they did so in immaculate three-piece suits.

Prince grasped the symbolism, understood the point Owen was trying to make – but still baulked at wearing a suit. Not in this lifetime, thank you. Instead, Prince would sit there silent in the meetings, exuding charisma, while Owen and Gary did all the fast-talking. It seemed to work too. Only Prince wasn't convinced. There was always a snag: CBS insisting they'd have to see him work in a studio before allowing him to pro-duce his own records; other labels talking about showcase gigs or financing further demos. There were lunches in big fancy Hollywood restaurants and a lot of talk of mansions in the Hollywood hills and round-the-clock limousines.

It wasn't until they met with Russ Thyret at Warner's, though, that finally things clicked into place for Prince. Russ was a genuine music man who had worked with Stevie Wonder, another exceptional black artist who had begun his career inconceivably young, and another brilliant singer and multi-instrumentalist with his own singular vision for how his music should sound. Eschewing the usual Hollywood hotspots, Ross took the meeting at his home, sitting around on the floor with Prince just talking music for hours.

Thyret *got* Prince. 'There was a real bonding there,' Husney later recalled. When Prince explained that he didn't see himself as a 'black artist' or a 'white artist', that he was neither rock nor funk, though his music incorporated both and a whole lot more, Russ merely nodded and agreed. The only snag was the stipulation that Prince produce his own records. He'd already turned down CBS for that reason. Walked away from a deal with A&M, too. Thyret got all that but could only promise he would give his strongest recommendation to his boss, Warner's legendary chairman, Mo Ostin.

Mo Ostin was 50 years old, and had worked with greats like Frank Sinatra, Ella Fitzgerald and Sammy Davis Jnr. In 1967, he had famously signed Jimi Hendrix after witnessing his incendiary performance at the Monterrey Pop festival. Since then he'd worked with Neil Young, Frank Zappa and Paul Simon. Ostin was old school, a proper record man with exceptional 'ears', in the vernacular of the biz, and well acquainted with the proclivities of star musicians. Nothing about Prince gave Mo pause for thought. Indeed, he was overjoyed to make another exciting 'find'.

When Owen Husney, Gary Levenson and Prince sat down to look at the deal Mo Ostin put before them, they couldn't believe their eyes. Ostin had instructed his team to go all in, offering this talented newcomer a deal worth a million dollars, albeit spread over several years, during which Prince would be expected to deliver seven albums, the first three within two years of signing.

Ecstatic, Prince duly signed to Warner Bros. on 25 June 1977, less than three weeks after his nineteenth birthday. Suddenly the frantic, frustrated teenager who would pick fights with people just for looking at him funny flip-flopped into a super-chilled young man with the world at his feet. As he later told *Rolling Stone*, 'Once I was eating every day, I became a much nicer person.' He was, he said, 'able to forgive'.

Years later, Prince would boast in the *Guardian*, 'We had to fight for over a year before I even got signed. So whatever I turned in, they had to accept. They weren't even allowed to speak to me!' Behind the scenes, though, Ostin and Warner's were now getting cold feet over the decision to allow Prince to produce his first album on his own. CBS had previously floated the idea of bringing in Earth, Wind & Fire's bassist, Verdine White, to produce the sessions. That had proved to be a deal-breaker. When Warner suggested they bring in Verdine's brother, Maurice White, to at the very least co-produce, Prince similarly freaked out, writing a lengthy letter to Ostin in which he made it clear to the Warner boss that there would be only one producer of his album – and that was Prince.

'I just turned down all the producers that Warner's suggested to me for the first album. Even when they finally agreed to let me produce myself they insisted I had to work with what they said was an Executive Producer, who was really just an engineer. And that caused a whole lot of other problems, because he was versed in shortcuts and I didn't want to take any – though that *was* why it took five months to make,' he added with a dark chuckle.

Eventually, after another senior Warner's figure, Larry Waronker, witnessed an early session for the song 'Just As Long As We're Together', the green light was finally given to Prince to produce. There was just one more thing Prince wanted, he told Waronker, before he left that day. 'Don't make me black.'

Waronker was shocked, he later told the *Star Tribune*. Prince had been lying on the floor as Waronker walked towards him in the studio to say goodbye. This was the clinching moment for Waronker, he said. The moment it became clear to him, as he put it, that 'we shouldn't mess around with this guy'. Prince insisted it wasn't just about musical stereotyping. It was because of a much wider personal philosophy. As he elaborated to Chris Salewicz, 'They say that even if you've just got one drop of black blood in you it makes you entirely black. But in fact I don't necessarily look on myself as a member of the black race – more a member of the human race.'

Prince finally began work in earnest on his debut album on 1 October 1977. Like its title, *For You*, this would be – for Prince, at any rate – a relatively straightforward affair. He may not have wanted to be marketed as a black R&B artist but the songs on *For You* rarely spoke of anything more.

Beginning with the 67-second title track, a celestial orgasm of sound, multi-tracked vocals cascading like a waterfall, before segueing into 'In Love', a mid-paced, sweet-lipped pop-soul confection, the first truly Prince moment comes with 'Soft and Wet', the track he'd co-written with Chris Moon. Nowhere near as lascivious as its title might suggest, and a universe of pop away from the real nitty-gritty that would swiftly follow on subsequent albums, it's an obvious choice of first single, which it became in March 1978, tiptoeing to No. 12 on the *Billboard* R&B charts. (In fact, the first single to feature the teenage Prince had been released the year before: a hard-driving funk workout titled 'Stone Lover' by a short-lived Minneapolis band, Music, Love and Funk (MLF). Prince picked up a session fee for playing on the track, which he used to help finance his trip to New York.)

The rest of the 33-minute *For You* was similarly pleasant, similarly fun, similarly tame; love songs sculpted into sweet-tasting grooves and birdsong harmonies; its most impressive feature, ultimately, the credit on the sleeve that proclaimed: 'Produced, arranged, composed and performed by Prince.' That and the 27 different instruments he had played on the record.

Released on 7 April 1978, unsurprisingly it was not a hit, squeaking into *Billboard*'s Soul Chart at No. 21, but barely scraping into the *Billboard* Top 200. There were few reviews, the handful of notices the album did get more impressed by his age and competency on so many instruments, a distinction Prince was already growing tired of, blanching at the word 'prodigy'. 'I don't even know what the word really means,' he insisted. 'I'm just a person.' Then when the Warner's publicist, Bob Merlis, against the odds managed to snag Prince an interview with the influential magazine *Record World*, he appeared to intentionally sabotage the interview by upsetting the writer, DeDe Dabney. 'She got through a few questions,' Bob recalled in *Billboard*. 'Then out of the blue he asked did her pubic hair go up to her navel. It was disconcerting.' After that, 'We thought maybe he shouldn't do interviews . . .'

It wasn't just Prince's questionable interview technique Warner Bros. were not happy with, though. Prince's contract had budgeted for $180,000 to be spent making his first three albums. *For You*, which took five gruelling months to complete, had cost almost as much as that on its own.

Nevertheless, Owen Husney went back to the well and pleaded for Warner's to pony up money for Prince to do a small tour. He would need a band so Warner's organized auditions in LA. But a moody and taciturn Prince refused to choose a single player. Instead he returned to Minneapolis and called André to come and be his bass player. André was thrilled and leapt at the chance. Then cousin Charles, who'd long since forgiven Prince for shooing him from his band, suggested a pretty girl named Gayle Chapman for the keyboardist's spot.

Talking about it in 2013, Gayle said she felt somehow that her joining Prince's first solo band was destined to be. She recalled: 'I was standing in my living room and I was listening to [*For You*] full blast. I was home alone and this still, small voice shot through my mind. It said, "In order to tour, he's going to need a band." I turned off the music and looked around. God had spoken to me.' She laughed. 'I'm not kidding. I mean, it was wonderful and spooky at the same time.'

When her chance came just weeks later she was more convinced than ever. Three months after her initial audition, however, Prince had not got back to her and so she gave up hope. Then one afternoon he rang, asked her if she could come to rehearsal – right now. Later, when Gayle asked Prince why he had hired her, he told her straight: 'You have blonde hair, blue eyes and you can sing. You're the funkiest white chick I've ever met.'

Prince hired Bobby Rivkin to be his drummer for similar reasons. Jimmy Harris – now Jimmy Jam – whom Prince had known since high school and had been such a feature in Flyte Tyme, tried out for drums but was ultimately rejected. 'I was the biggest Prince fan in the world. I thought he was *brilliant*. But I didn't make it.' Not yet anyway. Meanwhile, Bobby Z, as he became known (after his grandmother's nickname for him, 'Butzie'), was white – and Prince was determined to hammer home the message that what he did wasn't just 'black' music. That he was about that largely unexplored musical terrain where rock met funk – met jazz, folk, pop and whatever else Prince wanted to bring to the party at any given moment.

He also tried out other familiar faces from the local scene but not everybody was convinced enough to sign up. Sue Ann Carwell, a singer Prince had acted as an informal mentor for under her stage name of Suzy Stone, was invited to join but soon bailed out. 'I didn't really believe in Prince,' she said simply. Ricky Peterson, a talented keyboardist whose playing merged blues, jazz and rock in a way that strongly appealed to Prince, was offered a gig but turned it down after hearing Prince's strict ground rules: no drinking, no drugs, no turning up late. Peterson decided it sounded 'like a horrible boot camp' and walked away.

Eventually Prince found the guy he really needed in an old pal of Bobby's: Matt Fink. A tall, nerdy-looking guy whose musical tastes were almost as permissive as Prince's – Bowie, James Brown, The Who, Steely Dan – Matt was up on all the latest technology, adding his own ARP synthesiser to the growing collection of instruments Prince shared his apartment with. Matt was also another visual foil. On stage he would live up to his surname by dressing as a jailbird. Later, he would reinvent himself as Doctor Fink, sporting surgical gowns and a mask on stage. Matt could write too. He was in and would stay in for the next ten years.

'I always said I would play all kinds of music and not be judged for the colour of my skin but the quality of my work,' Prince once explained. 'I wanted my band to be multiracial, male and female – to reflect society.'

He decided he still needed one more addition to the live band: another guitarist, ostensibly to play rhythm, but some-one capable enough of doing more when called upon. An open

audition was held in a tyre shop with a backroom big enough
to hold the band and all its equipment. Prince arrived two
hours after the scheduled start time. A long line of would-be
guitarists had formed outside in the snow, all in a hurry to get
in out of the cold. One in particular pushed himself forward, a
23-year-old black cat begging that he only had 15 minutes to
spare because he had a gig to get to with his own small-town
band, Romeo, and could he please try out first.

Prince nodded him over and the young hopeful plugged in
and waited. Prince took his name: Desmond D'andrea Dickerson – Dez. Without another word the band began to chugalug
a rhythm, which Dez then began playing rhythm guitar to.
When Prince signalled for Dez to take a solo he did so, capably,
but without any attempt to try and outgun the obvious star
of the show. Prince was impressed. Finally he began talking
to him, checking out his background, music, attitude, then
he shook hands and wished him well. Got back to the other
people waiting. Then had Owen Husney call Dickerson back
later, offer him the gig.

By January 1979, Prince was ready to play his first show
with his new five-piece solo band. Warner's had assumed he'd
be making his debut at a showcase gig in LA or New York.
But Prince insisted instead on doing two shows back-to-back
at an old North Minneapolis movie theatre called the Capri.
He was so nervous before the band went on the first night he
could barely speak. Then the moment came and he took off
like a jet. Introduced onto the stage by a local DJ as 'the next
Stevie Wonder', in fact Prince did everything he could to come
on like the new Jimi Hendrix or Mick Jagger: tight jeans, shirt
open to the navel, waistcoat and a long raincoat flapping open,
waving his guitar around like a giant phallus. Anything not to

be confused with disco. 'To me disco was always *very* contrived music,' he explained later. 'It was all completely planned out for when the musicians were recording it in the studios. Basically, what *I* do is just go out and play.'

A review in the local paper, the *Star Tribune*, talked in typically tabloid terms of 'a royal future for Prince'. But the show was beset by technical problems and got a friendly but lukewarm reaction from the audience, which numbered less than 300. With the Warner's bigwigs flying in for the second night's show things would have to be ratcheted up a notch. With the equipment glitches sorted out, Prince really put on a performance for that second show, dancing and twirling and attacking his guitar like an angry lover. But the posse from the record company watched with their limo running outside and left as soon as the show was over.

Then the verdict came back the next day: Prince wasn't quite 'ready' for a full-blown tour, they had decided. He should keep working, refining his act. Maybe try again when he had a second album out and more original material to choose from. This time, Husney agreed, refused to fight them on it. And Prince lost faith. Began to question every move that had been made on his behalf until then. Maybe Owen wasn't the right man for the job after all. Prince informed Warner's he would need a new manager.

It seemed an abrupt move. Hadn't Husney gone out on a limb to support Prince when he had nothing? But for Prince, in those early make-or-break years, the only real loyalty was to himself. A shrewd music historian, he had seen what had happened to other artists who had been left to wither on the vine, one-hit wonders that hit a record company roadblock and never got past it. Prince didn't need a manager who sided with the record company. So he decided he would find someone new. It became a pattern of professional behaviour that would characterise Prince's entire career. Hiring and firing, to get to where he wanted. Prince was making history, he decided. Too bad for those left behind in its wake . . .

With the label ready to advance Prince $30,000 to make his second album, they moved fast to try and find him new management. They put him in touch with Don Taylor, who handled Bob Marley, but the day-to-day person Taylor assigned to deal with Prince, Karen Baxter, found Prince 'just too weird for me'. So they turned to Earth, Wind & Fire's management team of Bob Cavallo and Joe Ruffalo, who also had experience of working with Sly Stone, one of Prince's big influences. Unlike Baxter, Cavallo and Ruffalo immediately connected with Prince, and a deal was struck between them.

With new management came new thinking. Until then all the battles in Prince's career with Warner's had been about independence, who would produce and play on his albums, what kind of songs he should write, how he would be marketed. Prince had mostly got exactly what he wanted – and it hadn't really worked. This second album would have different priorities. He would still insist on producing it himself and playing all the instruments, but its focus this time would be much more on making it a commercial success. Retreating to his apartment, which he had now fitted with his own virtual studio, Prince began crafting what he hoped would be surefire chart hits. No more eight-minute epics. Not for now anyway.

One of the first songs he came up with under these new criteria was 'I Wanna Be Your Lover', an obvious smash hit from its effervescent opening groove. Originally written at the invitation of Warner's as a possible track for inclusion on the 1979 album *Pizzazz* by jazz singer-pianist Patrice Rushen, but she rejected it and Prince decided to show her what she'd missed out on.

Prince may have decried disco, may have gone out of his way to emphasise over and over that there was more to his music than the colour of his skin, but 'I Wanna Be Your Lover' was pure soul disco, a guaranteed pop hit whatever decade it had been released in. It was simply undeniable. The kind of track *everyone* loved, male, female, black, white, anyone with a pulse, basically.

Still Prince couldn't resist adding his own particular spice to the lyric, when he sings of wanting to be 'the only one who makes you come', quickly adding, '. . . running!' Before going on to sing about how he doesn't just want to be the girl's lover but her 'brother . . . mother and sister too'. Or, in other words, when Prince fucks you baby, he fucks every little bit of you. All done with that sugar-sweet falsetto that could melt mountains . . .

There would be other moments on the new album when Prince still went out of his way to underline his white 'rock' credentials too – most notably on 'Bambi', like Led Zeppelin meets the Bee Gees. But it was the upbeat downtown sound of 'I Wanna Be Your Lover' that would become the outstanding musical motif, including the other track from the album designated as a potential single 'Why You Wanna Treat Me So Bad?'

Another track originally written for Patrice Rushen but again rejected was 'I Feel for You'. Catchy as a cold, hip-swaying and upbeat, a love song at first gander, but again laced with something more, as the crux of the song revolves around the singer's careless admission that his love is 'mainly a physical thing'. Here, though, Warner's missed a trick, overlooking the song's commercial potential. Instead it would become a massive worldwide hit four years later for Chaka Khan, reaching No. 1 in the UK and No. 3 in the US, after the legendary producer Arif Mardin had fattened up the sound with the rapper Melle Mel, a wall of synthesisers and a sample of Stevie Wonder's beautifully chromatic harmonica.

Recorded back in LA, at Alpha studios, in Burbank, in the late spring of 1979, *Prince*, as the new album was simply called, though credited once again entirely to Prince, benefited enormously from the attentions of its engineer, Gary Brandt. Prince, he recalled, was 'reasonably open-minded' to his suggestions, and unlike *For You*, which had taken five painstaking months to complete, from start to finish *Prince* took barely four weeks.

When 'I Wanna Be Your Lover' was released as the lead single from the album, in August 1979, it immediately began demolishing pop and R&B radio stations across America. Jimmy Jam recalled: 'When "I Wanna Be Your Lover" came out, it was the best record I'd heard in my *life*!' Edited down to 2 minutes 57 seconds (from the five-minute-plus jam it extended to on the album), 'I Wanna Be Your Lover' opened the floodgates for Prince, going to No. 1 in the *Billboard* Soul Chart and reaching the dizzy heights of No. 11 on the national pop chart. Suddenly Prince was a pop star, and when the album followed in October it sold over half a million copies, climbing to No. 22 on the mainstream album charts.

Not all the critics liked it. Decrying it as neither fish nor fowl – its pop-rock sheen not as sleek and thrillingly revelatory as Michael Jackson's *Off the Wall*, which was No. 1 at the time, and nowhere near as cerebral as the latest wave of rock intelligentsia as epitomised by Talking Heads, whose *Fear of Music* was the 'thinking' white critics' funk-rock album of choice in the autumn of 1979. Prince and his bubbly pop-soul hit were a one-off, the general feeling went. Lightweight and fun but not to be taken too seriously.

As if anticipating this reaction, Prince had ordered his backing band into the studio with him that summer to make a more collaborative album. He even gave the group a name for the first time: The Rebels. The five band members could not believe their luck. Over the next 11 days they recorded eight tracks together, only four of which had been written by Prince, the rest by Dez and André. Gayle even sang lead vocals on one track, imitating Prince's falsetto on some decidedly 'questionable' lyrics, including the line: 'You, you drive a girl to rape.'

Everybody was excited when Prince told them of his plans to release The Rebels' album alongside *Prince*. Then just as suddenly the deal was off, the album never released, and the group idea abandoned completely. No explanation was forthcoming from Prince, certainly no apology. The whole thing was never mentioned again.

Instead Prince now pressed on with taking his band out on the road in support of *For You* and *Prince*. It had been a while coming but he was determined to make up for lost time. His first show in LA, at the small but prestigious Roxy club on Sunset Boulevard, also attracted his first big-time reviews, including a particularly astute notice in the *Los Angeles Times* by Don Snowden that read, in part: 'It must be a daunting prospect for anyone to make his or her performing debut . . . before an industry-heavy crowd at the Roxy.' But that 'Prince, 19 [*sic*], is something of a wunderkind who produced, arranged and composed all the material and played all the instruments on his two Warner Bros albums. His vinyl output, somewhat like Stevie Wonder's, is aimed squarely at the black-pop mainstream and crossover audiences but his live show is heavily influenced by hard-rock flash.'

The result, Snowden rightly concluded, 'is a bizarre combination of musical and visual elements. Guitarist Des Dickerson (black leather jacket and leopardskin pants) and bassist André Cymone (legs encased in plastic wrap) both look more punk than funk. Prince largely sticks to guitar and throws enough pelvic grinds and phallic guitar poses at the audience to give most obnoxiously macho rock stars a run for their money.'

The review went on to compare Prince's falsetto to that of Eddie 'Hey There, Lonely Girl' Holman, but said it lacked the power to cut it when the band more self-consciously tried to rock out. It noted that the audience was 'largely black' and that Prince's most pressing problem would be how to 'straddle two disparate musical worlds' – a point underlined further when his next single, the more rock-oriented 'Why You Wanna Treat Me So Bad?' missed the *Billboard* Hot 100 completely and stalled at No. 13 on the R&B chart.

There was a definite buzz building though and Warner's were able to capitalize on that by getting Prince and his band booked on two enormously influential mainstream TV shows: Dick Clark's Saturday morning pop show, *American Bandstand*, and, a few weeks later, the much hipper musical-comedy variety show, *Saturday Night Special*. The latter was a triumph, get on, do your thing, get off again. Thank you and goodnight. But the Dick Clark appearance would go down as one of the most cringe-making moments in pop TV history when Prince simply refused to answer any of Clark's innocuous questions.

Years later, Prince's friend Pepé Willie claimed the singer

told him he simply froze on stage under the pressure of having to act witty in front of the glare of the TV cameras and the watching millions at home. 'He said, "Pepé, it all hit me at one time." He got stage fright. And at that time he said to me, "That will *never, ever* happen again."' According, though, to Dez Dickerson, the whole thing was planned after Prince had taken a dislike to Clark in a pre-show meeting in the green room. A PR ruse that worked brilliantly, Dez felt. 'Dick Clark still talks of it today.'

Suddenly, Prince was being treated like a star. Something that he had planned for and dreamed of since he was a boy banging away on his father's piano. Now it was happening, though, he was adamant in interviews that nothing had really changed in his life. 'If I lived in California and rode around in limos all the time with people waiting on me hand and foot, then maybe that could make you change. But I'm not into all of that,' he told one writer, a theme he elaborated on later, in a lengthy interview for the influential music paper *New York Rocker*, explaining how 'when my first album came out I used to watch the charts, but I gave up on it after that. It became so . . . see, you can look at the charts and you know for a fact that your record is better than some of the things that are over you. But I could look at it objectively and realise why those records were ahead of mine, that it's all basically business politics.

'I just now started to meet some of the radio guys and the promo people. Originally I didn't want to do any of that, because it was basically a stroking game and I didn't want to get involved in it at all. Now that people have seen us, though, I think they're genuinely into it – and I don't mind meeting people who really dig us, rather than, "Well, this cat gave me a television set so I'm gonna play his jam, and it's been nice meeting you."'

He did admit that the wider public was now starting to look on him as something else, something far beyond his own reckoning. 'People that know me basically stayed the same – we'll be friends to the end. I guess. People that don't know me – they pop out of everywhere now, all these so-called friends who remember me back in school. A lot of people say that the person who goes through it all changes, but I don't think that's true. I think it's everyone else who changes, because they expect certain things from you and they'll approach you in a different manner. As far as moving is concerned – I can't stand LA, so I would never live there . . . Every time I have to go out there I dread it. It's that attitude of everybody – I lose sight of what I'm doing when I'm there, it's like a dream factory . . .. They spend so much money! They make it and spend it, and for crazy reasons . . .'

Fine words, but Prince and Warner's were about to spend money for what many would conclude were crazy reasons to try and refocus Prince's career trajectory, which would, they hoped, maximize the same two markets Prince had been yelling about going for from the beginning: the black R&B crowd and the white rock audience. The early months of 1980 would see him opening for the funk-rock superstar Rick James at enormous arenas across America, with Prince playing his own cherry-picked shows in each town at whatever new-wave venue was available. The reasoning: that Prince would be playing to two different crowds in every town, hopefully attracting a firm following amongst both.

Rick James was, like Prince, a black artist who had achieved a toehold with white rock audiences due to his multi-instrumental skills with guitar, keyboards, bass and drums. Ten years older than Prince, he was already an established star in America, plying much of the same onstage shtick Prince would grow to call his own. Indeed, James later claimed that throughout their 38-date arena tour together, Prince would stand at the side of the stage watching Rick perform, 'remembering everything I did, like a computer'. By the end of the tour James was dismayed to note how much of his act Prince had now adapted into his own performances, flipping the mike stand back, cupping his ear during audience call-and-response set pieces, even, he said, the way he was 'stalking the stage'.

James became pissed off, ordered a hotel room showdown between the two bands, at which he later claimed Prince backed down 'like a little girl'. Certainly, Prince toned down the James steals for the rest of the tour. But while James would years later talk of the 'respect' and affection he held for the younger man, he didn't bother to conceal his contempt while they remained on tour together, recalling in his memoir how at the end of tour party he had snuck up behind a seated Prince, forced open his mouth and poured a glass of whisky in it. Prince, who had never drunk alcohol, spat it out and stormed off furiously, as James and his entourage looked on and laughed.

The tour with Rick James was starting to rub off on Prince in other, more positive ways too, though. The songs he started writing in his hotel room, or jamming with the band at sound checks, also betrayed a distinctly James-like raunchiness. One of them he began showing the others, 'When You Were Mine', was a catchy pop-rock anthem and sounded like it could have been written specifically for James. While another, provocatively titled 'Head', showed Prince was now willing to up the ante. To go where no black or white rocker had ever gone in their songs before: to the bedroom and beyond. Way beyond . . .

4

Dirty Boy

London, Lyceum Ballroom, 2 June 1981. The place is barely half full but the people that are here are clearly out for a very good time. An illicit confection of eyelinered Blitz kids, jazz funk smoothies, new wave refugees, even a few soulboy purists looking somewhat lost, wondering where the disco mirrorball is. This is not the kind of mainstream pop and rock audience the Lyceum has grown used to playing home to on a so-called normal Tuesday night. There is even, over there in the corner, looking as though he's now regretting the idea, a tall white boy sporting stockings and suspenders, high-heeled shoes – and a long dirty mac.

And me. It's probably fair to say that none of us feels entirely at home. After all, most of us have never been to a Prince concert before and actually for once we really don't know what to expect. Looking at the cover shot on his latest album, *Dirty Mind*, it's even harder to predict. A black guy (or white mixed-race guy, it's hard to tell even from a picture) dolled up like Phil Lynott from Thin Lizzy – but without his trousers on. Just a thong. Oh, and black stockings.

Prince would explain the extravagant garb away as merely functional in interviews from the time. The stage clothes only looked strange, he felt, to 'people who only read about it . . ., but I think the people who come to see it already expect it and wanna get into that. I've gotten a lot of criticism from outsiders, but once they see the show they understand why I wear what I wear. The show's real athletic and we run around a lot, and I have to be real comfortable. The decision was left up to me, and when I thought about what I was most comfortable in, it's what I sleep in . . . I just can't stand clothes.'

The tracks on the album were, at first acquaintance, just as confusing. What *was* Prince playing? Funk? Rock? Disco? Dance? *A musical striptease?* All of the above, or indeed none? The only thing for sure was that, like its title, the album was absolutely filthy. No question. One listen and it was time to change the sheets, baby.

For this, once again Prince had been almost deliberately misunderstood – or perhaps, this time, far too easily understood – by the beard-stroking critics who ruled the roost over the British music press. Ian Penman of the *NME* offered up the most pretentious putdown of the Lyceum show when he wrote, tongue surely up the cheeks of his arse: 'For a wolverine habitué of the sharper clubs and bars of our capital such as myself, this tawdry "gig" was something like a step into the horrors of Hieronymous Bosch from the accustomed gilt-edged decadent sumptuousness of Klimt!'

For me, as a jobbing young music journo out most nights of the week at club gigs where the possibility of finding music you could actually tap your toe to was as rare as hen's dentures, Prince at the Lyceum offered a wonderful change of pace. Not quite as startling as the show I'd seen him perform at The Ritz in New York the previous December, but definitely something different – and fun. That had been on my first visit to the city that never sleeps and *Dirty Mind* was one of the first albums I'd been given and told to pay attention to when I arrived. Listening to it on cassette in my hotel room overlooking Gramercy Park, *Dirty Mind* made perfect sense. The driving rhythm, the overly permissive use of guitars and synthesisers, the yelping vocals and, yes, the naughty songs. This, it seemed to me, was exactly what New York was supposed to be about. Loud, lewd, risqué, unapologetic – and screamingly, unforgivably *dirty*.

The official Warner's press handout said it best: *'Behind the frequently shocking lyrics is a deep belief that by removing the taboos and allowing youth to express its sexuality in all its forms, we will achieve a more wholesome society.'* I wasn't entirely sure about that last part but you know what they say: when in New York (for the first time) . . .

Then I saw him and his band perform at The Ritz and I really got it. This was funk-rock-sex music not a million loft-parties from what Lou Reed had been talking about for the past decade, right? Then when I was introduced to Prince, oh so briefly, after the set at The Ritz, by one of the over-eager team from Warner's, I felt like I'd just accidentally walked into the room where all the burlesque dancers unashamedly run around naked as they get changed, their eyelashes flapping thunderously from all the heavy makeup. By the time he'd finished his set, Prince was all but naked save for the eye-wateringly tight black knickers and thigh-hugging stockings he wore. He was now draped in a gown but you still felt as though you were intruding in his boudoir. He smiled demurely as we spoke, though avoided direct eye contact, offered a very limp wrist when we shook hands. I felt we got on well though, had a moment there together, then realized afterwards he had barely said a thing worth writing down.

'You're from England? Uh-huh . . .'

Next thing, he'd vanished. Someone said he'd left to get back to his hotel, as the band was travelling the next day. Someone else said he was in another, more private room backstage, being entertained by some female fans. Others that he simply had this trick of appearing and disappearing whenever he felt like it.

The show at the Lyceum was similar if somewhat more subdued. The only difference was that by then I'd fully absorbed the *Dirty Mind* album. At a time when the UK was either still in thrall to the New Romantic pop ideal – *NME* – or rediscovering its caveman roots with a new wave of British heavy metal acts – *Sounds* – Prince and his dirty *Dirty Mind* album found it hard to find a home. Yet for those of us that had fallen for its lascivious, fun-poking grooves, it marked the beginning of what we felt sure was to be a fascinating musical journey for this boy-girl, black-white, rock-funk . . . creature.

Just as he had with *Prince*, most of the songs and ideas behind *Dirty Mind* had been worked out long before Prince began recording. If *For You* had mainly been about seeing what happened when Prince made his dream come true – the sheer exhilaration of finally making his own album overtaking the need for strict quality control – and *Prince* had been mainly about showing he knew how to write and record hit songs, the third Prince album was to be a whole new mission statement. Something bold and out there that Prince could really turn into a live show that showcased *all* his talents.

The other major change was that this time Prince would not be making the album in LA, under the noses of Warner's execs. 'We built him a studio in his house in Minneapolis,' recalled a Warner A&R rep, Ted Cohen. 'That's where he made

Dirty Mind. He could record twenty-four hours a day.'

Prince knew he didn't have an obvious hit single this time. No 'I Wanna Be Your Lover' to prop up sales and draw the mainstream audience in. He'd done that. Now it was time to make his move. It was as if the first two Prince albums had been the boy struggling to find his true musical identity – and *Dirty Mind* was what happened now he'd become a man. That was certainly how the astute *Rolling Stone* reviewer, Ken Tucker, saw it when he wrote: 'He takes the sweet romanticism of Smokey Robinson and combines it with the powerful vulgate poetry of Richard Pryor. The result is cool music dealing with hot emotions. At its best, *Dirty Mind* is positively filthy.'

Or as Prince later put it: 'I've always written real explicit . . . I don't think sex is dirty at all. I think it can be described as anything just as soccer can be described.' Certainly all the songs seemed to have a one-track mind. Not love songs, so much, as pure s-e-x. On 'Uptown', the twist is when the girl looks at him and asks: 'Are you gay?' and he replies, nonchalantly, 'No, are you?' Not that it mattered because they were going to get it on anyway. They weren't going to let society 'tell us how it's supposed be'.

Nor were they on 'Do It All Night', where this time the girl 'may have had good sex' with guys like Fred and Fritz and Sam and Max, or 'been a slave' with a whole bunch of other guys (Tim, Tom, Ed and Dave, seeing as you ask), but she was never going to feel as free as when she was 'doing it with me'. Most controversial of all was 'Sister', with its unambiguous lines about an older sister who 'never made love to anyone else but me' and was the reason 'for my, uh, sexuality'. Was this guy kidding? Putting us on? With Prince, you never really knew.

Then there was 'Head', about his seduction by a bride-to-be

– actually in her bride's gown – who simply insists on sucking his cock before leaving for the wedding, ending up with his come on her fancy white dress. All set to a body-pumping beat and a repeated chorus of: 'Head! Till you're burning up. Head! Till you get enough!'

Prince later recalled how most of *Dirty Mind* 'was done right there on the spot, writing and recording. That's how a lot of the stranger lines came out . . . the swearing and like that – it's basically what I was feeling at the time.' He admitted that even his management weren't sure about some of the songs. 'They said, "The sound of it is fine. The songs we ain't so sure about. We can't get this on the radio. It's not like your last album at all." And I'm going, "But it's like *me*. More so than the last album, much more so than the first one."'

In fact the tracks that so taxed both Prince's management and his critics – and Warner's – were only the tip of an iceberg that had found Prince writing almost stream-of-consciousness lyrics to songs that didn't make the album, like 'When the Shit Comes Down', 'Big Brass Bed', 'Eros' and 'Rough'. Warner's didn't know what to make of it. This was not what they had expected as a follow-up to *Prince*. But with this being the last album of his initial three-album contract, Prince no longer felt the need to pander to the whims of, as he put it, 'record company mama-jammas'. Never mind that this didn't sound like he used to, this was what he sounded like *now*. Dig? So determined was he to shift perception away from the doe-eyed newcomer with the talent bigger than his trousers – away from the cutesy child-star Stevie Wonder thing and nearer to the gangland band thing of Rick James and, most telling at this point, Cameo – he even gave an extra credit on the *Dirty Mind* sleeve to one Jamie Starr, credited as 'engineer'. But Matt Fink gave the game away when he later explained that that was just Prince not wanting to seem 'like he did *everything*'. Prince wanted it to seem like he had a whole band thing going on. A whole gangbanging party!

The other new thing about *Dirty Mind* went largely unrecorded at the time, or if it was mentioned at all it was done in such a derisory fashion as to make it seem like one more thing about Prince to dislike or misunderstand: the sudden idiosyncratic spelling of song titles and lyrics, using 'U' for 'you' and '2' for 'two'. These days of course almost everybody in the Western world does the same with text-speak. Back then it simply looked weird and unnecessary, like Prince was just trying to draw even more attention to himself – which was precisely the point.

Warner's were so worried about how *Dirty Mind* would be perceived: Stevie Wonder had signalled his progress from boy to man with some of the most 'conscious' soul music ever made; even Michael Jackson had made his play for creative adulthood under the tutelage of Quincy Jones, the classiest act in the biz. Why did Prince have to attempt the same leap from boy to man by talking such trash? Incest? Threesomes? Banging some babe in her wedding dress? Come on!

Indeed, so put out were Warner's they even slapped a sticker on the promo copies of *Dirty Mind* that went out to radio station programmers: 'Audition Prior To Airing'. If that wasn't like saying, 'Don't play this, you're not gonna like it', reasoned Prince, what was? Yet still he refused to tone down the songs – or his photos and live performances. When record store owners also then baulked at allowing the album prominent shelf space because the picture on the cover was simply too suggestive, it meant record sales would now be affected. Not because the cover shot was of a near-naked Prince – but because he was in those damned black panties and thigh-length boots and dirty-old-man raincoat.

The overall message, however, did at least get through. No more was there any confusion over what 'genre' Prince could easily be slotted into. The answer was: he couldn't. Wouldn't. Don't you dare try and make me! Instead, Warner's began talking him up as a new-wave artist. One whose arch, 'ironic' lyrics were perfectly in keeping with the daringly risqué mien of the most cutting-edge bands. Kind of like Cameo, the pioneering New York funk band whose breakthrough 1980 album, *Cameosis*, had been an influence on Prince, and Material, another band from New York who were adding a new, post-punk electronica to their hard street funk.

In truth, though, sections of Prince's band were also starting to doubt the new, potentially divisive direction his music was taking. Gayle Chapman, blonde and pretty and deeply religious, was fine with it – until Prince devised a set-piece on stage during 'Head' whereby she was to come out from behind her keyboards, get down on her knees before the grinning singer, then bend over backwards as he walked over her while still playing guitar. Or on other occasions miming playing keyboards on her stomach. When, on two occasions, the movement ended with Prince French kissing his keyboard player, Gayle had a change of heart. She left the band.

When in the years to come she was asked if she had left because of the onstage antics of 'Head', Gayle would laugh it off. 'Yes, I did tell him that I did not want to sing that song ['Head'], but I sang "You". So what?' She sang the lyrics: '"You get so hard I don't know what to do." How stupid was I? "Take your pants off!"' She burst out laughing. 'No, I really digress

. . . I wasn't growing. I was in a band, touring, and it was the most fun I had in a long time . . . But I needed more and I couldn't put my finger on what it was. I just knew I had to go.'

Gayle's replacement would be Lisa Coleman, a cute-looking 20-year-old Mexican-American from LA. Lisa came with a musical pedigree. Her father, Gary L. Coleman, had been a well-known session player in the Sixties and early Seventies – part of the vaunted LA collective known as The Wrecking Crew, playing vibraphone and various percussion instruments on everything from the soundtrack to the musical *Hair*, to Simon & Garfunkel's *Bridge over Troubled Water*. Gary's fellow traveller in The Wrecking Crew and good friend was Mike Melvoin. Mike's daughter, Wendy, was Lisa's best friend growing up, once saying, 'We've been familiar with one another since we were in diapers.'

Lisa was just 12 when she got her first paid job as a musician, playing keyboards in a teeny bop outfit called Waldorf Salad. A kind of me-too Partridge Family that featured various Coleman siblings plus Wendy Melvoin's brother Jonathan. Signed to A&M the group only lasted a couple of years. In 1975, Lisa landed a small role as a high school pianist in a Linda Blair TV movie.

A graduate of Hollywood High, the secondary school whose showbiz alumni included Lon Chaney Jr, Judy Garland, James Garner, Micky Rooney and Lana Turner, to name just a few, Lisa was a smart, talented young woman, used to being surrounded by hyper-talented creative types. She'd been studying for an English degree at LA Community College when she dropped out after just a year and began teaching piano. A tip-off from a friend who worked at Prince's management office led to her making a demo tape and sending it in.

Intrigued, Prince invited Lisa to come and play at his 16-track home studio. Lisa got his attention immediately when she began playing a Mozart concerto she'd recently been learning – at the speed of a rock song. They began jamming, Prince on guitar, Lisa on keyboards, and she ended up spending the weekend in his spare room. A purely platonic relationship: Lisa made it clear she was already involved with somebody – Wendy Melvoin, as it turned out, whom she would have a serious relationship with for the next ten years – something Prince not only respected, but would use to his advantage when Wendy also later joined his group. Lisa later recalled how during a photo shoot for a *Purple Rain* poster, the band were all lined up and posing when Prince 'walked over to me and Wendy and lifted my arm up and put my hand around Wendy's waist and said, "There." And that is the poster. That's how precise he was about how he wanted the image of the band to be. He wanted it to be way more obvious. We weren't just the two girls in the band.'

Lisa loved the idea of joining Prince's band. She was different. She'd always known it. Now here came the most 'different' band she'd ever come across. Certainly the songs she was asked to play on the *Dirty Mind* tour were not run of the mill. As she told *Rolling Stone*, 'I got solace from the fact that here were some other people so different that they only fit in there.'

In a brilliantly insightful interview that Prince gave to the English writer Chris Salewicz, published the week of the Lyceum show, we got the most complete portrait yet of the artist as a (dirty) young dog. Chris, a veteran of the black music scene who was on personal terms with Bob Marley, was neither overly impressed when he met Prince in New York that

Above and right Dirty boy. Prince in his earliest, most outrageous incarnation, 1981 (Top: Getty Images; Bottom: Photoshot).

Left, below and right Signs of the times. Top left: *Purple Rain* poster (Alamy). Bottom left: Prince makes love to the stage (Photoshot). Right: Never knowingly underdressed, Prince in 1990 (Getty Images).

Prince as the gigolo in *Under The Cherry Moon*, 1986 (Photoshot).

Above right Sheila E and Prince. He looked across the stage and mouthed the words: 'Marry me' (Alamy).

Right Prince proving it's not just girls who rule his world but his male dance troupe too, circa 1992 (Alamy).

Alphabet suit. Prince in Jimi mode onstage, circa 2001 (Photoshot).

Above right Prince on stage flanked by his soon-to-be wife Mayte Garcia (Photoshot).

Right Symbol, as he is now known, and Mayte, the most beautiful girl in the world, as she is now known, circa 1994 (Alamy).

th SLAVE stenciled in eyeliner across his cheek

summer, nor indeed overly critical. Chris got Prince and his deliberately in-your-face new album in a way that encouraged the 22-year-old to open up about his life and art in ways he never had before.

'I haven't been to sleep for a couple of nights,' Prince announced as he sat down. 'Well, I've been to bed, but not for sleeping,' he deadpanned. Chis eyed him ruefully. 'Ho, ho, ho,' he deadpanned back, miming nudging him in the ribs.

Prince immediately cut the shit. When asked about the new *Dirty Mind* album, he said of the ferociously upbeat music, 'I used to be a perfectionist – too much of one. Those ragged edges tend to be a bit truer.' The only lyric Chris took the young Prince to task over was the line on 'Sister' about incest. Was Prince saying he'd really slept with his older sister? 'I write everything from experience,' he replied. '*Dirty Mind* was written totally from experience.' So he had actually experienced incest, asked Chris? Prince shot back. 'How come you ask twice?' Then quietly chuckled to himself.

Eventually, though, the interview settled into a more revealing exchange, when finally they got around to talking about the things that really mattered to Prince. Starting with his ongoing struggle for musical identity. 'I think I've always been the same. But when you're in the hands of other people they can package it in a way that is more, uh, acceptable. All along I've had the same sort of ideas that came out on this record. It's just that my former management had other thoughts about it all.'

He went on: 'We also had long talks about what I felt was me getting closer to my real image, and at first they thought that I'd gone off the deep end and had lost my mind. Warner's basically thought the same, I think. But once I told them that this was the way it was, then they knew they had no choice and they'd have to try it, because they weren't going to get another record out of me otherwise.' He paused then added, 'I know that *I'm* a lot happier than I was. Because I'm getting away with what I want to do. With the other two albums I feel I was being forced to suppress part of myself – though also I was younger.'

Asked about his contemporaries on the American music scene, Prince sighed. 'All the groups in America seem to do just exactly the same as each other – which is to get on the radio, try to be witty, say the most sickening things they can think of and gross out the interviewer. They think that's going to make them big and cool.

'They're a little too concerned,' he went on, 'with keeping up the payment on the Rolls-Royce when really they should be busying themselves with doing something that's true to their own selves. Obviously the new-wave thing has brought back a lot of that greater reality. There are so many of those groups that there is just no way many of them can make it in those vast commercial terms. So they have no choice but to write what's inside of them.' Another pause. 'I think it's all getting better, actually.'

Salewicz then moved the conversation onto politics, of all things. Did the guy in the thong and thigh-boots have any thoughts on that? As it turned out, he did.

'Thank God we got a better President now,' he said, referring to the then recent election of Ronald Reagan. Reagan, said Prince unequivocally, had 'bigger balls' than his predecessor, Jimmy Carter. 'I think Reagan's a lot better. Just for the power he represents, if nothing else. Because that also means as far as other countries are concerned. He also has a big mouth, which is probably a good thing. His mouth is his one big asset.'

Sex, politics, music . . . it was all based on the same kind of riff to Prince. The one that could be played at any tempo, any melody and any beat, as long it always spelled the same thing: personal freedom.

'When I started doing my own records,' he told Salewicz, 'I really didn't want to listen to anybody, because I figured I should just disregard what anybody else might be doing. Though I suppose subconsciously I might have been influenced just by the mood that was going on around me. I can only be a product of my time.' Another thought, a half-smile. 'Unless,' he said, 'I cut myself off totally. Though that is soon to come.'

Baffled, Salewicz inquired what Prince was intending to cut himself off from exactly?

No hesitation. 'The world.'

And what would he do then? 'Just write music, and things like that. Hang around in my head. And just make records. I don't think I'll perform any more. I don't want to do this too much longer.' But why? He looked like he was having so much fun up there. 'It's still fun. But I get bored real fast. Yeah, it's still fun. But I can't see it going on for too much longer in the same fashion.'

It's hard to imagine that someone who would soon be recognised as one of the most exciting and innovative performers in the world was ever seriously contemplating giving up playing live. Prince, though, had already moved on to other enticements. He may have had a last-minute change of heart about The Rebels, but he still harboured the idea of forming some sort of band that he would not be a touring member of but would pull the strings for, creatively, promotionally, image-wise and sound-wise.

He decided this make-believe outfit would be called The Time and he set about writing and recording songs for 'them' to record. He also invited the rest of his band to contribute material. Lisa came up with one called 'The Stick'. Dez came up with a couple: 'Cool' and 'After Hi School'. Prince, who had such a backlog of unreleased material he didn't know what to do with it, added 'Oh, Baby', from two years before, to the notional Time set. Only André refused to play ball. He had other ideas for what he wanted to do with his songs, still hurt perhaps by the unexplained quashing of The Rebels. André had his own side project going which he was calling The Girls.

Prince chose to disregard this snub – at least, for now. He and André went back a long way. They were brothers. But like all brothers their love for each other could be stretched to its limit sometimes. Instead, Prince ran with the idea of The Time, making a proposal to Flyte Tyme to reinvent themsleves. They had always been the Minneapolis band that held the edge over Grand Central and Shampagne, at least in Prince's mind. But they had never quite broken out of the Twin Cities. So he decided to give them a break. He would write and create the music. They would be 'The Time' and perform it live – and, crucially, take all the credit on paper for all the songs, the look, everything.

The band, weary of playing the same tired Minneapolis circuit, was enthusiastic. Prince said there would be a major label deal to back it up, something Flyte Tyme had never come close to achieving. They said yes – with just one exception: their singer, Alexander O'Neal. Alexander was a straight-up dude with a great voice and his own stage presence. His dream was not to be another man's puppet, which is how he perceived the offer from Prince to front The Time. He wanted to be recognized fully in his own right. If he'd been mulling over a move towards becoming a solo singer already, now was the time, he decided. Alex told Prince he was out.

So Prince had a brainwave and invited Morris Day to come and be the singer of The Time instead. Morris it was who had allowed Prince to take one of his original songs and revamp it into 'Partyup' for *Dirty Mind*. Prince had offered $10,000 to let him have that track. But Morris had held his tongue and said he'd rather have a record deal. Now Prince was able to make good on his promise. Only one snag: Morris would have to follow Prince's instructions to the letter.

He agreed. But Morris had some ideas of his own too. He'd known Prince since their Grand Central days and knew not to hit him over the head with them. When he started talking about this hot new guitarist he knew from Rock Island, Illinois, named Jesse Johnson, he waited for Prince to start asking about him before suggesting Jesse might be the perfect guy to play Prince's guitar parts in The Time. Jesse was like an alternate version of Prince, a clairvoyant guitarist who could summon all the ghosts of rock and soul past. He'd made his bones when he had the audacity to quit the hottest black band in town for a white rock band – because the rock band played more gigs and made more money – and because he could replicate those iron-hard AC/DC riffs and purple-hazed Hendrix histrionics better than any man alive – showing his class at a local biker bar in front of the local chapter of Hell's Angels. When Morris called him about Prince and The Time, Jesse took it in his stride. You name it – black, white, all shades between – he could play it backwards. He got on the next plane to Minneapolis and The Time settled into its first 'real' line-up of Day, Johnson, Terry Lewis (bass), Jimmy Jam (keyboards),

Monte Moir (keyboards), and Jellybean Johnson (drums)

Morris may have got his way, making Jesse an integral part of The Time. But not before Prince had got everything he wanted out of the group: above all, total obedience. This nearly brought the whole deal to its knees when Morris broke down in tears, telling Lisa he simply couldn't keep up with the vocal styles and work rate Prince was demanding of him. Prince was not a great teacher. He had all the skills and knowledge and ideas waiting to be passed on, he just didn't know how to sell it to lesser beings other than to keep hitting them over the head with it until finally – finally – they got it just the way Prince wanted it.

Prince eventually recorded six tracks as The Time, with Morris on lead vocals. Three of them were over eight minutes long but even these had so much commercial potential they could easily be edited down as singles for radio, which two of them were: 'Get It Up' and 'Cool', both of which would soon hit the *Billboard* R&B Top 10. When Prince played them for Warner's execs out in LA, they rejoiced. Prince might have turned his back on the cream-and-sugar sound of 'I Wanna Be Your Lover', but here was Prince in another guise delivering exactly the kind of fun-times, no-edges R&B they felt they could purloin into a hit. They agreed to sign The Time on the spot. It didn't hurt either that by the terms of his contract Prince was now in a position where he could, if he wanted, tout his next album to other record labels. Warner's had invested a great deal in their child protégé, only to see their investment come enticingly near to paying off big time. They gambled that the best was yet to come – signing The Time would not only bring them a more commercially viable project than the one Prince was currently offering as a solo star, but it would keep him happy and encourage him to re-sign his contract with them.

This he did. When the self-titled debut album from The Time was released in July 1981, Prince kept his word about doing everything he could to let The Time claim ownership, even using a pseudonym on the credits, which listed its producer as 'Jamie Starr'. When the album reached the R&B Top 10 and No. 50 on the mainstream album chart he was as delighted as if it were one of his own albums in the charts – which, in essence, it was, of course.

His mission accomplished with The Time, at least for now, Prince immediately set about making his own next album. There was to be no let-up from the direction he'd boldly taken with *Dirty Mind*. This time the album was called *Controversy* – the Warner's team braced themselves for what they could expect. But once again Prince surprised them. Yes, there were tracks like 'Jack U Off', 'Sexuality' and 'Do Me, Baby' that would have fitted perfectly on *Dirty Mind*. But this time the rest of the album would take a more serious, more 'conscious' turn – at least, musically.

It seems Prince hadn't been joking when he told Chris Salewicz about his admiration for President Reagan. 'Ronnie, Talk to Russia' was a stroke of musical and lyrical politicking that would have made Sting proud: a rat-a-tat-tat dance-athon with speeding-bullet guitars that urged Reagan to get in the ring with Russia and talk peace, 'Before it's too late.'

On 'Annie Christian', meanwhile, the music starts out sounding like a malcontent Kraftwerk before Prince loses all cool and lets his guitar throw fire, railing against the child murders in the American south that were then making TV news headlines. And then there was the brilliant title track itself: self-aware, self-effacing, self-motivating, almost daring the listener to try and dismiss the track as just another one of Prince's naughty numbers, right up to the moment when he recites the Lord's Prayer entire, when in fact the suspicion was very much that lines like *'I wish there were no black and white / I wish there were no rule'* were about something far more interesting, even important.

Musically, the spastic, robotic rhythms of *Controversy* were so far removed from the sound of his first two albums it was hard to believe, on first hearing, that this was the same artist. All drums and percussion were electronically produced, with Bobby Z only making an appearance on one track: 'Jack U Off'. Where most artists looked on the new technological inventions like the Lin drum with suspicion, Prince embraced them. He adored the 'dead' drum sound the Lin produced. He wasn't interested in trying to make them sound like 'real' drums. He wanted to create something new with those cross-pollinated electrical pulses.

Nevertheless, with the exception of the genuinely thrilling title track, which reached No. 3 on the R&B charts but stalled at No. 70 in the national pop chart, there wasn't an obvious single on the new album. Nevertheless, Warner's accepted *Controversy* at face value and set about releasing it in September 1981. Prince geared up to tour heavily again, only now he was presented with another last-minute problem when André announced he was leaving to pursue his own career. Prince said he had seen it coming. Though when André then revealed he would be working with Owen Husney as his manager, there was fury behind the scenes. Prince was such a controlling person he could only have seen André's departure as a kind of rejection of Prince himself, which of course in many ways it was.

Speaking sometime later, André listed a number of reasons for his departure: claims that Prince took credit for one of his songs, and that he also denied him a sleeve credit for singing and playing on his first three albums, even that it was he, André, that had actually got The Time together. 'I never wanted to be a solo act,' he said in *Creem* magazine, in 1985. 'I would have stayed in that group, but I enjoy playing in a happy environment with musicians who enjoy playing with each other. And that wasn't the case in Prince's band.'

Ouch. Not that Prince was going to let anyone think he cared. Instead he immediately hired another familiar face from back in the day – Mark Brown (aka Brown Mark) who had played bass in another bunch of good-not-great Minneapolis scene-makers called Fantasy. Prince called Mark and offered him the gig, on one condition: Brown would have just two weeks to find his groove in the band. If things were not all smoothed out and working well by then, he would be sent packing again. Brown swallowed his fear and simply said yes. What else could he say? By now no one was daring to argue with Prince about anything.

5

Two Thousand Zero Zero

With the title track picking up some radio play, *Controversy* became the second Prince album to make the US Top 40, peaking at No. 21. But the tour was still a relatively modest, cost-conscious affair, the group and its roadies travelling in three station wagons, the equipment judiciously packed into one van. Ted Cohen was again along for the ride, doing his best to get interest for each date from its local radio stations. Cohen, who'd worked with several big-name artists, including Fleetwood Mac and The Who, was knocked out by the shows. Prince was, simply, 'the embodiment of everything that made rock'n'roll cool and everything that made soul cool . . . It was unbelievable. You weren't ready for how good he was.'

When one writer asked Ted to describe a show at the Santa Monica Civic Center, he smiled and replied, 'There wasn't a dry seat in the house.' Backstage the vibes were loose, upbeat, he recalled. 'We hung. We spent a lot of time together. The band was very close. Prince didn't isolate himself.' The only thing he refused to do for Ted was record store appearances, after the first one in San Francisco went badly awry. 'A girl reached over and scratched his cheek and that was the last in-store he did for twenty-five years.'

Opening for Prince on the *Controversy* tour was The Time.

To ensure they were on top form by the time they joined the tour in November 1981, he sent them out on a series of small club shows down South, on what used to be called the chitlin' circuit – venues that specialised in black performers. Jimmy Jam recalled the band being mightily disgruntled. 'I lost it. "We've got a record on the charts. Where are the girls? Where are the screaming crowds?" Prince planned it like that, so we'd get our performing skills together.' That all changed once The Time joined Prince on tour. Screaming girls, hangers-on, yes-men, suddenly they were surrounded by them. 'There were all kinds of undergarments thrown onstage for Prince,' Jam recalled, 'not so much for The Time.'

With Prince writing almost all their material, at this stage only Morris Day received the occasional co-writer credit, and both Jimmy Jam and bassist Terry Lewis were becoming frustrated by that. The two had been the principal creative members of Flyte Tyme. Still in their early twenties, they itched to flex their creative muscles once again, especially now they had a well-selling album behind them. The other members of The Time, though, were happy simply to be enjoying some measure of success at last.

Jam remembered: 'At the end of the *Controversy* tour, we were sitting around a hotel room, just the Time members, and Terry said, "I want to go to LA and make some demos. They need us out there." And this will mark the time for you – everybody's answer to Terry was, "Man, you're crazy. I'm saving my money for a VCR." A VCR! So I said, "Terry, I'll go."' Although Jam and Lewis would stay for another two albums by The Time, it was the beginning of the end of their association with Prince. Prince may have been utterly promiscuous in his own wish to make music with a variety of different musicians, but there would be hell to pay for any of them under his creative wing who dared try the same thing.

But that was all to come. In the meantime came some news that really stunned Prince. The Rolling Stones wanted him to open for them at a series of high-profile shows at the massive 92,000-capacity LA Coliseum. Prince had recently been trying to explain his vision for his own band as being 'like a black Rolling Stones'. But he was frankly stunned when Mick Jagger let it be known that he personally would like Prince to open for the real Rolling Stones. Jagger always had good antennae. Had a remarkable habit of always co-opting whoever was currently upcoming and hot to the Stones' cause, particularly when it came to helping sell tickets for their huge shows. In the late Sixties he'd done it with Ike & Tina Turner and BB King, later in the Eighties he'd do it with Guns N' Roses. In 1981, it was Prince's turn. Jagger had also been present at the Ritz show the previous Christmas and had been keeping a weather eye on Prince ever since.

Prince would be bottom of a bill also comprising the Stones-alike J. Geils Band and blues-punk favourites George Thorogood and the Destroyers. But it was still Prince on the same bill as the Stones. The new black Jagger, as Prince liked to think of it, versus the original white one. It was an almost too perfect way to kick off the *Controversy* album and tour.

What could possibly go wrong?

The answer: almost everything.

It should have been the fillip to the *Controversy* tour that turned it into a sell-out. Instead the two shows Prince performed opening for the Rolling Stones at the Memorial Coliseum in Los Angeles, in October 1981, became the first real disaster of his career.

Prince may have already been a star with black American R&B audiences; may have stated his case with the white new-wave crowd that dominated the music press in Britain and Europe. But any notion he had that he was also making inroads into the consciousness of hardcore American rock'n'rollers was destroyed the moment he took to the stage at the Coliseum for the first time.

On a sweltering California day, before a boozed and hairy crowd that had been there since the gates opened at 6 a.m. and was now impatient to have Mick Jagger and the self-styled 'greatest rock'n'roll band in the world' come on and rip off their heads, the sight of this largely unknown – to them – figure bopping about the stage in his crotch-hugging underwear and long trenchcoat was like a red rag to an angry bull. The fact that his band appeared to playing *disco music* further enraged the crowd. (This at a time, it should be recalled, when disco was considered the antithesis to everything righteous and groovy in album-oriented rock.)

Sensing the mood Prince ended the opening number 'Uptown' prematurely and immediately changed the set, ordering the band to go straight into the more foot-stompin' 'Bambi' from *Prince*. He also changed his singing voice from the pleading falsetto of the studio original back into his much deeper speaking voice, and climaxed the song with a long, louder-than-hell guitar solo, yelling, 'Rock and roll California!'

But when two songs later they sprang 'Jack U Off' on the Coliseum rockers, pandemonium broke out. Most of the 92,000 crowd had never heard the song before and a great many thought he was singing, 'Fuck you off!' Immediately the stage became the target for anything and everything the crowd could get their hands on: fruit, beer bottles, shoes – even an open packet of chicken giblets.

Prince was distraught, bringing the show to an abrupt halt after just 15 minutes, leading the band off the stage to sustained booing from the crowd. Back in the tent that doubled as his dressing room, he wept, vowing he would never share a bill with the Rolling Stones again. 'I'm sure wearing underwear and a trench coat didn't help,' he admitted, 'but if you throw trash at anybody, it's because you weren't trained right at home.' He flew back to Minneapolis the same night, telling his management to cancel the second of the two shows he'd been booked to perform at the Coliseum. Even when Jagger phoned and spoke to Prince personally, he still refused to return for the second show. It was only when Dez called and began reframing what had happened less as a musically prejudiced event and more as a racially motivated slur that Prince reconsidered. 'You can't let them run you out of town,' Dez told him. Prince was on the first flight back to LA the next morning.

The second show was another disaster. News of Prince's collapse the previous day had filtered out and the second day's crowd was determined to join in the fun. The result was an even more excruciating spectacle as Prince and his band suffered even more slings and arrows. Only this time Prince did not flounce off the stage, did not throw in the towel: instead, he delivered a full-on performance. When it was all over, though, it was agreed that he should pull out of the handful of other dates on the Stones tour he had been booked for. And Prince made himself a special promise: that he would never open a show for anybody ever again. A promise he kept for the rest of his life.

In fact, the debacle of the Stones shows would become

a major turning point for Prince. If it's true to say that we learn more from our losses than we do our wins, this was the moment Prince truly pledged to up his game and take his music and career to a vastly higher level. The moment when he stopped kidding himself he could really be taken seriously as some kind of outer-limits artist who indulged himself in music, clothes and ideas designed primarily to attract attention – seemingly at any cost.

Now he began to plan a more significant move. A double album that would retain the admiration and respect of his existing fan-base, containing all the daring and risqué mystique he had become known for – but one that would also go several steps further, lifting Prince onto a whole new plateau, from which he would look down on the rest of the music world for ever more.

He would no longer tolerate not being the biggest star in his universe. When The Time began to get better reviews than even he did on the *Controversy* tour, he dropped them from the bill for certain high-profile shows where he knew the media would be out in force. He would never abandon them: Prince was as delighted as anyone when their debut album went gold in America for over half a million sales. But he refused to play second fiddle. Instead he turned his immediate attention to yet another side project: an all-girl group built around a stunningly beautiful 23-year-old former model from Canada named Denise Matthews.

With Polish, German and Jewish ancestry on her mother's side, and Afro-Canadian, Hawaiian and Native American blood on her father's side, Prince considered Matthews the most exotic-looking creature he'd ever seen. Matthews, for her part, was convinced Prince was gay – until he took her out on a date, at which point, she said, 'I realised he was definitely *not* gay.' Prince had been toying with the idea of calling his new all-girl group The Hookers. As soon as he met Matthews, though, he came up with a better idea. He would change her name to Vagina – pronounced Va-gee-na – and put her front and centre of a group also comprised of his friend Susan Moonsie and Brenda Bennett, his wardrobe lady. There would be no instruments, just the girls singing and rapping while dressed up in sexy lingerie and high heels performing neo-erotic dances to the songs Prince would write for them. There would be few live shows, their promotional medium focused almost entirely on videos and TV appearances.

Fortunately for Matthews, within weeks Prince had cooled on the name Vagina and renamed his new queen of the scene, Vanity – and the group Vanity 6. Coming up with a song a day for eight days, with occasional help from The Time's Terry Lewis – 'If a Girl Answers (Don't Hang Up)' – and Jesse Johnson – 'Bite The Beat' – and one full song – 'He's So Dull' by Dez Dickerson – Prince played all the synths and electronic drums on the record, as well as producing it (this time under the pseudonym The Starr Company) even contributing a co-lead vocal with Vanity on 'If a Girl . . .', affecting a wry 'lady voice'.

Once again Warner's was only too pleased to sign Prince's latest project, releasing the self-titled album in August 1982, replete with a front cover depicting the girls in suitably come-hither outfits. Following in the wake of the success of their 'Nasty Girl' single and video, the *Vanity 6* album would reach No. 45 in the *Billboard* Hot 100 mainstream chart. Plenty of room for career development. Only this time, unlike his commitment to The Time, Prince's passion wavered and, though Vanity 6 would be included on the bill for Prince's next American tour, by 1983 Vanity had turned against Prince, angry and humiliated that he was now bedding both her and Susan Moonsie. By the end of the tour in 1983, Vanity was travelling alone in her own tour car, and when it was finally over Vanity 6 was also no more.

Prince, meanwhile, had completed work on a second album for The Time, titled *What Time Is It?* – after one of Morris Day's onstage catch-phrases (and later to become a full-blown Time song in its own right). Released simultaneously with the Vanity 6 album, and again featuring Prince on almost everything, bar Morris Day's honeycomb vocals, like its predecessor it only boasted six tracks, but four of them were lengthy funk-jam tracks – and of a much higher quality than the largely improvised stuff on their debut. As a result, *What Time Is It?* snuck into the lower reaches of the US Top 30, eventually going platinum for over a million sales. It even boasted a genuine hit single, with lead-off track '777-9311' reaching No. 2 on the R&B chart – the title actually Dez Dickerson's real home number, causing his phone to ring off the hook for weeks afterwards until he finally got it changed.

Prince was on a roll and Warner's were more convinced than ever to keep bankrolling whatever project he brought them next. What Prince had in mind for his next album though was something he had already decided was too good to simply give to someone else. Still stinging from the Stones public shaming, perhaps, now more determined than ever to double-down and go for broke, he added to his home studio, upgrading it to 24-track, and began piecing together the most substantial set of material he had ever come up with in one go.

With so many of the songs recorded on the hoof – often in

the middle of the night when his band members were either out somewhere or fast asleep – he began experimenting more with computers in his search for something new to bring to his sound. The robotics of *Controversy* were already sounding dated, the more loose sound of The Time proving there was still an audience for a more fulsome, organic approach – even if most of it would come from his own small-hours experimentation with computerised sound.

There were early tracks like 'Let's Pretend We're Married', an elongated mechanical groove given flesh by Prince's promise to 'Fuck the taste out of your mouth'. Working for 72 hours at a time, there were a string of similarly lengthy Time-like jams. The big turning point came, though, with a song he wrote after waking up from taking a nap in Lisa Coleman's pink Ford Edsel saloon. It was called 'Little Red Corvette' and when it was released as a single in February 1983 it would become Prince's biggest hit yet, reaching No. 6 in America and No. 2 in the UK, selling over a million copies along the way.

First, though, came an even more triumphant moment in the song that became the title track of the new album: '1999'. A song ostensibly about the futility of war and therefore the more urgent need than ever to dance the night away, what '1999' really represented in the minds of the new generation of Prince fans who bought it in its millions, and, more importantly, had their eyes peeled open with delight at the ostentatious video that lit up the screens of the still new and full-of-fun MTV, was the sound of the future – two decades ahead of time.

It really did feel like that, from its spectacular keyboards and percussion grand entrance to the enticing first lines which Lisa Coleman positively purrs into the microphone: 'I was dreaming when I wrote this, forgive me if it goes astray . . .' to the starburst guitars and vocals as Prince dances and twirls around in the mix, his most impossible-to-ignore musical moment since 'I Wanna Be Your Lover', but delivered at a sonic velocity far exceeding those comparatively humble beginnings. Forget the previous attempts to meld genres, funk with punk, rock with rhythm, soul and roll. This was future pop, spaced out and spruced up and glittering like shooting stars colliding all at once.

The reviews were also spectacular this time around, as though the 'serious' critics had finally caught up with him. Writing about *1999* in *Musician*, Laura Fissinger declared that *1999* found 'Minnesota's palace darling [making] it quite clear, thank you, that his gifts are even less modest than he is. Profundity and innovation are now regular houseguests; sex is his version of Joseph Conrad's sea and Bruce Springsteen's all-night drive. And I dare you to find a better dance-floor sexmeister.' While in *Creem*, the doyen of American rock journalism, Richard Riegal confessed that 'the album that *1999* most suggests to me is *Electric Ladyland* [by Jimi Hendrix] in the way the four sides don't obey any grand thematic design, as much as they just get it up in your face with potent gem after hidden gem'.

It wasn't just the music, though, that now had the media in thrall. The video set the template for Prince's image for the rest of his life. The bare hairy chest now concealed beneath a white frilly-necked shirt, the black knickers replaced by more colourful, stylish trousers. And, most significantly, the long trenchcoat now gave way to another knee-length coat, but this one bright shiny purple. ('He was never going to give up on the long coat,' claims one insider who doesn't wish to be named, 'as it gave his tiny body length and shape. He was always very self-conscious about his lack of stature, shall we say.')

With the band now augmented by the presence of Prince's new girlfriend, the 20-year-old blonde beauty Jill Jones, pictured in the *1999* video dressed in stockings and suspenders and high heels sharing backing vocals with Lisa Coleman, the two young women spooned together at the keyboards, it was this far more glamorous, sharp-dressing and fun image that helped propel Prince onto the front pages of magazines like *Rolling Stone* for the first time: a real flag-waver for the *1999* album – a double – which was released in October 1982 and eventually sold over three million copies.

When the 'Little Red Corvette' single came out early in 1983, with the *1999* tour in full swing and the album still burning up the chart, the accompanying video – shot at the same filming as *1999* and featuring the same red-lit set, the same shiny new purple coat and frilly white shirt, though no girl-on-girl action at the keyboards to titillate this time, the focus more on Prince's raunchy dance moves – became one of the first videos by a black artist, along with that of Michael Jackson's 'Billie Jean', released the same month, to be placed on 'heavy rotation' by MTV. When the most pop moment on the album, the impossibly catchy 'Delirious' quickly followed it into the singles chart, Prince found himself an MTV fixture. Such was the popularity of his sexy videos that a fourth 'unofficial' video was later shot, this time for the eight-minute opus 'Automatic', using the same-looking set, but with Prince in a purple jacket this time, and bikini-clad Jill Jones returning to nestle alongside Lisa at the keyboards – but as a single it was only released in Australia, and as such was viewed as a rarity.

The *1999* album was no less of a triumph. Only 11 tracks, but with four of them stretching way past the seven-minute mark, this was Prince at once unashamedly commercial and artistically adventurous at the same time. There were environmental songs – 'Something in the Water (Does Not Compute)' and a punchy six-minute epic called 'All the Critics Love You in New York', which Prince considered one of the best songs he'd ever written – part Lou Reed downtown putdown, part Bowie in Berlin whiteface, part supercool space dude. And of course there was also Prince's by now trademark sexual fantasies set to pure bump and grind. 'Horny Toad', the B-side to his 'Delirious' single, led with the line: 'All I want is to whip your body until it bleeds'. 'Lady Cab Driver', another album standout, features the protagonist punishing the female cabbie for her unbridled S&M sexploits, as well as – apparently – starting a war and chastising him for the fact his brother is 'so handsome and so tall'.

With the two biggest-selling albums in America in 1983 being Michael Jackson's *Thriller* and Def Leppard's *Pyromania*, *1999* seemed to straddle both sides of the black–white divide, rock with soul power, R&B with new improved technology, a wave so new it was now out there on its own, waiting for whatever Prince decided to do next with it. The question was: how could he possibly top that? The quite brilliant answer would come soon enough.

First though, Prince had a new problem on his hands: fame. Not just notoriety or music press infamy, but real, everyday man-in-the-street fame. Suddenly it wasn't just the music press that were writing about him, it was heavyweight newspapers like the *LA Times* demanding interviews. And lined up behind them every tabloid magazine and newspaper in the world, it seemed. Genuinely taken aback, Prince did what he always did in times of fear and confusion – he took off. Vanished.

Then announced he would no longer be giving interviews – to anyone.

It was also around now that Prince hired someone who would become an ever-present figure at his side for the next few years: Charles Huntsberry – Big Chick, to his friends. Chick was 6 feet 8 inches tall and weighed 400 pounds (approximately 28½ stone). If that didn't make him stand out enough, he also sported a long white 'Father Christmas' beard. Chick was a former professional wrestler who had worked in law enforcement in Tennessee before moving on to private security work for stellar rock bands like AC/DC. Now, he would become Prince's personal guard. Prince admitted that at first Chick scared even him. But at Dez's urging, Prince kept him on and quickly grew to like and trust him. If Prince no longer wished to commune with the press – or indeed anyone outside his growing entourage of trusted friends and co-workers – Big Chick was the amiable giant guaranteed to protect him.

A former tour manager, Alan Leeds, later recalled the Prince of this time being 'suspicious and paranoid of people and life in general, and sarcastic and cynical and clearly troubled by his personal demons. The more we learned about his background – the kinds of rejection he suffered as a youngster – it certainly didn't add up to a very secure, well-rounded individual.' Another former aide-de-camp from those days recalled that 'When he was angry, his eyes could burn you and you were scared'. While yet another reckoned: 'His expectations of people are unreasonable and that's why the relationships end up disappointing both sides. He uses them up and spits them out – not in a nasty way, but just because people can't keep up with him.'

Jimmy Jam and Terry Lewis certainly felt the full force of Prince's wrath when it emerged that they had been moonlighting, producing an album on the quiet for the LA electro-funk outfit S.O.S. (aka Sounds of Success). The band had hit it big with their debut album, *S.O.S.*, in 1980, but their two albums since then had been commercial duds. When Jimmy and Terry were invited to come in and not just produce but co-write the next S.O.S. album, *On the Rise*, released in 1983, they jumped at the chance. The problem was they were already on tour with The Time, who were opening for Prince on his *1999* tour. Taking advantage of a four-day break in New York, Jam and Lewis flew down to Atlanta to work in the studio with S.O.S.

As Jam recalled in *Billboard* in 2016: 'Prince had told us, "Don't go produce other bands". He didn't want us to give away The Time's sound.' But when the two men were stranded at Atlanta airport because of snow, and were forced to miss the next stop on the *1999* tour in San Antonio, Prince fined them $2,000 – even though, according to Jam, they were only being paid a weekly tour salary of $170 at the time. When the tour was over, Jam and Lewis flew to LA to continue work on the S.O.S. album – and were surprised to get a phone call from Prince, also unexpectedly in LA, requesting an urgent meeting.

When they arrived they were met by Prince and a maudlin-looking Morris Day and Jesse Johnson. Prince came straight to the point: he had warned them not to produce other artists. But they had gone behind his back and done exactly that. That left him no choice but to fire them. 'I sat there for a second and then walked out,' said Jam. 'Terry stayed for a little while and tried to reason with him.' But it was no use. One of the worst affected, though, was Morris. 'He was very depressed about it, because he felt like The Time should be his band and he didn't get to make the decision.'

In public, however, Morris was still Prince's biggest advocate. Interviewed by *Creem* magazine halfway through the *1999* tour, Day made his position absolutely clear when he boldly stated that 'Prince was the only one who was man enough to let us out. There were a lot of people even more established than Prince who didn't want to follow us [on stage] so we had trouble getting on a tour. What we're doing complements what Prince does. We're both doing something new and I go along with the idea that maybe he brought us out to make it clear that what he's doing isn't as totally out of whack as it would seem if he were the only one doing it . . . we're making a new sound. I think the Time is a lot cooler than Prince, but we're the same kind of people. I can't speak for Prince, but I'd like to think that our music is sexually motivated. We do what we sing, we're cool, we get it up . . .'

Even Jimmy Jam would later become reconciled to what had happened to him. 'At the end of the day [Prince] was the boss and he was paying the bills. At the time we only saw it as us trying to improve ourselves. We weren't trying to leave The Time but if you're a creative person you want an outlet for that creativity.' He added: 'Looking back on it, I now realise that you can't criticise the boss unless you *become* a boss. When that happens you begin to realise the decisions that are made are made on economics.' The whole experience touring with Prince had been a once-in-a-lifetime trip, he said. 'It was such a learning experience. The road life was everything it was cracked up to be and more. This was before the days of AIDS – or so we hope! – and it was very much about the whole groupie scene. We were never into the drug thing but the girls were *crazy*! It was everything you'd fantasise about being famous. Women would just throw themselves at you!'

Prince's sphere of influence was now growing so fast, it seemed nothing could touch him. As the English musician and writer David Toop would write in a memorable essay titled 'Black Rock': 'Prince's achievements, setting aside his musical brilliance, should be commonplace by now: a mixed race, mixed gender band, playing psychedelic rock funk that appeals to white and blacks (though not enough blacks for Prince). The fact that this is still unusual, despite the increasing crossover of white and black markets, is remarkable.'

Quite so. Yet there was no denying that it was this less easily processed meeting of music and image, of low ideas and high ideal, that was now propelling Prince to the very forefront of eighties music, whatever musical genre – or cultural cul-de-sac – you cared to try and define him by.

Rock stars other than Mick Jagger were also now dropping Prince's name into their interviews, one of the more amusing comments being made by The Who's guitarist and leader, Pete Townshend, who now only half jokingly compared Prince to Chopin. According to Townshend, Prince was 'an indisputable giant genius who is only going to appear in context over the next two or three hundred years . . . it's just demoralising. Not only is he running a studio and a band and writing songs and playing great guitar and dancing, but he's obviously lifting weights and doing aerobic training. Where does the guy fit in his extraordinary sex life that I keep reading about?'

Rather than show fatigue, however, Prince was now aiming higher for his next project. The rest of the band had noticed that on the tour bus he would spend the time travelling between shows writing away earnestly for hours at a time in a big yellow legal pad. They knew it couldn't just be lyrics Prince was writing. He tended to come up with those more spontaneously, and would polish off a whole song in less than ten minutes sometimes. What *was* he up to?

Finally, he pulled aside Steve Fargnoli from his management team and explained what he had in mind. After five albums, this last his most successful yet by far, Prince was impatient for a new adventure. It would still be about the music – for Prince that was a holy sacrament – only now he had a new idea of how to present it. On record, yes, obviously, on stage, yes, always. But first though, for his next album, would come something entirely unexpected – a Prince movie!

Fargnoli didn't know what to say. He may have been part of a highly experienced music management team, but he knew nothing of how you went about making a movie. He told Prince this but the singer brushed it off. He was going to make a movie, come what may, all Steve and his team had to do was go out and get a deal for it from a major movie company. Simple dimples.

Fargnoli promised to do his best then fretted and sweated through a series of hard-knock meetings in which he was virtually laughed out of the room of every meeting he managed to arrange. None of the movie studio execs he pitched the idea to considered Prince a bankable movie star. The kid had had, what, one big album? Come back in five years . . .

Finally, in desperation, Fargnoli's partner, Don Cavallo, did what they had done with every other side project Prince had dreamt up these past three years: he took it to Warner's chairman, Mo Ostin. As far as Prince was concerned, Ostin told Cavallo, Prince was in a good place. So far everything he'd brought to the company had made money. Now with *1999* he'd achieved his first multi-platinum sales and even cracked MTV. Prince wanted to make a movie built around whatever his next album was going to be about?

Sure, why not? Mo didn't even ask to see a screenplay. He loved Prince. Knew in his dedicated music man's heart that he was still only at the start of his journey as a superstar. Don't worry about a thing, he told Cavallo. Mo Ostin would loan Prince the money to make his movie out of his own pocket. Would that keep the kid happy?

It would. For now . . .

6

Purple Reign

Up until 1984, the history of rock stars starring in movies had been chequered, to put it mildly. Elvis Presley made 32 movies of which at least 30 were considered duds. The Beatles made five movies during their lifespan as a group, all highly entertaining to Beatles fans but of limited interest to serious moviegoers. Bob Dylan had taken a minor role in *Pat Garret & Billy The Kid*, and been scorned for it. Everyone else – from The Monkees to Kiss, to Marc Bolan and Pink Floyd – had been largely eviscerated for their efforts. There were some great 'rock movies' – *The Girl Can't Help It, Easy Rider, Jubilee* – and some immersive documentaries – *Woodstock, The Concert for Bangladesh, The Last Waltz*. The only movies made though featuring a major rock star in the lead role that received serious and sustained critical attention had been *Performance*, starring Mick Jagger, and *The Man Who Fell to Earth*, starring David Bowie.

What on earth did Prince think he could bring to the table with his movie that would place him in the latter, more exulted category? The answer was simple: Prince would bring himself! What could possibly be more interesting than that?

He was in for a rude awakening though when he first met the movie's 23-year-old director, Albert Magnoli. When Prince asked Magnoli what he thought of the script, which Prince had written himself, Magnoli told him simply: 'I think it sucks.' Still new to the business – he had only graduated from the Film School at the University of Southern California two years earlier – Magnoli had immediately identified the chief weakness of Prince's initial script: although it was essentially an autobiographical story about his life as 'The Kid', it was too internalised. It failed to address 'the musical culture of Minneapolis – Prince and the Revolution, The Time, that whole scene'. There was a movie to be made here but saddled with that script it would 'not work in a million years'.

Requesting a video compilation of Prince's performances, to try and see a way around the problem, Magnoli was even more downcast. 'The video was depressing. He was so unpolished. I thought about calling it off. On the way to the airport I asked the limo driver, a young black guy, if he knew Prince and what he thought of him. 'Isn't he a fag?' he said. So now I've got that on my back too.'

Eventually, in the early hours of the morning, Prince drove Magnoli out to a spot 'in the middle of nowhere, where I thought he might kill me'. Instead, he looked at Magnoli and asked him why he was so sure about the changes he wanted to make to the movie.

Magnoli recalled: 'I said, "Let me ask you, if I have the father punch you in the face in the first five minutes of the movie, is that okay?" He asked why, and I said, "Everyone on the planet wants to punch a rock star in the face." He laughed, saying, "Yep, I understand that", and I said, "Let's go make a movie."'

The next step was to help Prince choose which of over 100 songs he had written for the movie would work best. Together, they eventually picked 12, partly based on the music – Prince

– partly based on how the lyrics could help form parts of the dialogue or help different scenes segue into the narrative. It was this process that brought 'When Doves Cry' to the fore-front – a track not everyone had been convinced by as it came without a bass line. In Magnoli's hands, though, it would form part of one of the most impressive montages in the film.

The only track not from the original 100 songs Prince submitted for consideration was the one that would provide both the starburst climax to the movie when Prince wrings every drop of emotion from his guitar, and gives the film its enig-matic title, *Purple Rain*. Magnoli had first heard Prince play it during a benefit show for his friend Loyce Holton who ran the Minnesota Dance Theatre, held at First Avenue, the down-town Minneapolis nightclub where so many scenes in the movie would later be filmed.

By then Magnoli had become Prince's shadow, following him around trying to get a better idea of the real scene Prince now inhabited, at least in his hometown – the very thing that would give the finished film its air of authenticity, of reality. Decades before the advent of what we now know as 'reality TV', *Purple Rain* would invite its audience in to see every dif-ferent side to the real-life Prince that Magnoli could capture on film. The fact that Prince's 'fictionalised' celluloid version of his story also happened to be so glamorous – and downright sexy – as he rode around town on his purple motorcycle, ac-tually reflected only a portion of the real-life adventures the principal star was now having, both in front of and a million miles away from the cameras. The fact was Prince was always *on*. The movie just emphasised how much so.

The end result, released in July 1984, was an instant, worldwide success, shooing *Ghostbusters* from No. 1 at the

American box office and sending Prince's star into the strato-sphere. Certainly it was the most fun, go-see movie in America that summer: ideal for dating couples to get their groove on to; perfect for single males and females to whirl and twirl to as they fantasised about escaping into their own parallel purple universes.

Teased by the simultaneous release, a month earlier, of the *Purple Rain* album and its commanding single, 'When Doves Cry' – the latter replete with the ultimate in movie trailers as its MTV-saturated video – both of which went to No. 1 in America and the Top 5 in the UK and every other country in the world. The weeks leading up to the release of the *Purple Rain* movie had been a magisterial procession, with the second single from the album, 'Let's Go Crazy', with its dizzyingly exciting intro – Prince pointing from his purple pulpit, 'Dearly beloved, we are gathered here today . . .' – also going straight to No. 1.

Many film critics were sniffy over the movie, calling it preposterous and self-indulgent. Missing the point entirely: this wasn't something aimed at cinematic posterity – the plot, such as it was, saying less than the music. Prince plays The Kid, leader of The Revolution – an amalgam of everything the real-life Prince had done up to then – while the great instru-mentalists – with the leggy Wendy Melvoin now taking Dez's place on guitar – were enhanced by state-of-the-art technology and synchronised bump'n'grind dance routines straight out of black vaudeville. All 'teeth and asses' as Morris Day's charac-ter – named, uh, Morris Day – explains at one point.

As in real-life, Prince & The Revolution find their place top of the bill at First Avenue threatened by the upstart Day and his equally entertaining group of funk-rock misfits, The Time.

Morris also does his best to 'make time' with Prince's new girlfriend – on film and in real life – Patty 'Apollonia' Kotero by putting her in her own group. There are also scenes of Prince trying to keep his father, a frustrated piano player, from beating his white mother. The dialogue is mainly one-liners and the modest budget gives the whole thing a slightly claustrophobic B-movie feel. The performances though are electrifying.

Here was a genuinely hotwired rock'n'roll movie for the MTV generation, heavy on musical – and sexual – ecstasy, refreshingly light on intellectual mannerisms. It helped if you were still young at heart when you watched it. It helped more if you didn't take yourself – or Prince – too damn seriously.

One reviewer who did get it, though, was the future Pet Shop Boys singer, Neil Tennant, who wrote in *Smash Hits*: 'The atmosphere of the film is compelling. A deep, musky sexiness hangs in the air throughout.' Before concluding: 'As a "rock film", it is very ambitious and far superior to most with its frantic concert scenes. And for what it reveals about Prince, it is fascinating.' The fans – old and mostly new – certainly thought so. *Purple Rain* would gross a worldwide total of $156 million, and would reward its star with an Oscar the following year for best original song score.

The *Purple Rain* album fared equally well at the box office, reigning at No. 1 in America for a staggering 24 weeks. For a few short weeks during that spell it meant that Prince held the No. 1 spot simultaneously in the singles, albums and film charts in America. Something not even The Beatles had ever managed.

Musically, it was also a major triumph, Prince's first overtly rocking album, most of the 15 million people who bought it being middle-class white kids who'd been just as eager to buy the other big rock hit of that summer, Bruce Springsteen's *Born in the USA*. As if to underline its street cred, three of its nine tracks – 'I Would Die 4 U', 'Baby I'm a Star' and 'Purple Rain' – were all based on live recordings from the Dance Theatre benefit show in 1983, with extra overdubs and vocals added in the studio. Indeed, the latter, with its soft-focus, almost spoken-word intro building towards a cathartic chorus set alight by its orgasmic guitar crescendo finale, was destined to become the 'Stairway to Heaven' of the 1980s.

For the poppy 'Take Me with U', a duet with Apollonia, Prince had to coach his girl, who'd never sung before, through her lines. At first he tried getting her to vocally strut along to the Vanity 6 hit 'Sex Shooter', but it was too much for her. Eventually he got a useable take out of her and they ended the session laughing. At the same time, another newcomer on the scene was also starting to get a lot of Prince's attention. Sheila E – short for Escovedo – was the daughter of Peter Escovedo, a renowned Latin percussionist. Just 21 when she first met Prince backstage at a show in 1978, she was already making her way as a percussionist in her own right.

Prince was instantly attracted to Sheila but she was wary, having just come out of a serious relationship with another famous musician, Carlos Santana. Santana had asked her to marry him – only for her to discover he was already married. Prince remained friends with Sheila for the next few years. When Sheila went on tour with Marvin Gaye, her hotel room would be festooned with fresh flowers every night – sent by Prince. When her next gig was with Lionel Richie, Prince joined her on tour, again as just a friend, though he never stopped trying to win her over.

Eventually, Prince persuaded Sheila to join his growing

stable of stars, recording her own album with him, *The Glamorous Life*, in 1984, which he produced and wrote the title track for (the latter originally intended for Vanity 6) – and which became a US Top 10 hit for her. He also rehearsed her for the video – transforming the simply dressed soul princess into a sexy vixen in a low-cut dress and furs, her dark hair gelled into a pompadour not unlike his own. She even twirled at the mike like Prince. When the *Purple Rain* tour opened in Detroit, Sheila E was the opening act. During the first few weeks of the tour the two finally became lovers. So began an on-off affair that would continue for the next three years.

It seemed Prince could simply do no wrong. This was just his time. He was not only the biggest star in the world, he could make you a star too. For the man with the purple-lit Midas touch, the plaudits just kept coming in. *Purple Rain*, decided *Q*, then Britain's biggest-selling and hippest rock magazine, 'exploded the Rick James cock-funk template and debuted the Sly'n'Hendrix "do" Kraftwerk disco rock incarnation.' You kind of knew what they meant – even when you didn't. 'Like Hendrix, Prince seems to have tapped into some extraterrestrial musical dimension where black and white styles are merely different aspects of the same funky thing,' claimed the review of the album in *Rolling Stone*. In the end, it would be left for posterity to really nail what lay at the magnificent heart of *Purple Rain*, the *New York Times* pronouncing it in the days that followed his death 'glorious, ecstatic, piercing, with anthems of quiet desperation ("When Doves Cry"), boundless energy ("Let's Go Crazy") or both ("I Would Die 4 U"). Though the album was designed as a soundtrack for the film of the same name, it stands as one of the most important records in pop history.'

Meanwhile the same mainstream pop audience that was about to gobble up 21 million copies of Madonna's own 1984 classic, *Like a Virgin*, also felt comfortable digging Prince's unisexual rock-pop-funk-punk-disco-Frisco-LSD-be-my-bb approach. For pure pop romanticism there was nothing as gorgeous on Madonna's album as 'The Beautiful Ones'. Nor was there anything as explicitly turned on as 'Darling Nikki', a 'sex fiend' Prince first meets in a hotel lobby, 'masturbating with a magazine'. Prince was also a much better dancer than Madonna.

And, even more controversial, when 'Darling Nikki' suddenly became the focus of media attention, in the wake of the decision by a then little-known Governor's wife named Tipper Gore (whose husband, Al Gore, would years later become Vice President to Bill Clinton, and, still later, a leading global-warming campaigner) to challenge Prince's, or any other musician's, right to include a track with such explicit lyrics on records aimed at young people.

The problem began when, in May 1985, Tipper had picked up her daughter's copy of *Purple Rain*, and was appalled by the lyrics to 'Darling Nikki'. Masturbation? With a magazine? What kind of filth was this? Within two months, Mrs Gore and 15 other so-called 'Washington wives' had formed the now infamous Parents' Music Resource Center (PMRC), a lobby group backed by Christian fundamentalists and partly funded by ex-Beach Boy Mike Love. They petitioned the Recording Industry Association of America, insisting that record sleeves remain free of obscene lyrics and that offending albums sport a coded rating according to sex, violence, drugs, alcohol or occult references.

The Association rejected such specific demands, but agreed

to voluntary stickering for generally explicit lyrics. Three months later, before a Senate hearing on pornography in rock, an eloquent Frank Zappa suggested this self-censorship was a political move in return for a tax levy on blank tapes and he slammed the PMRC for violating First Amendment rights on freedom of speech. Zappa's unlikely co-defenders included John Denver and Dee Snider of Twisted Sister, both victims of a PMRC black list that appeared to have initially been targeted mostly at heavy metal acts. The stickering debate was soon dismissed as a sensational media sideshow, however, though the labelling of LP and CD sleeves would continue.

Undeterred, seeing the threat of a warning sticker on his albums as almost a badge of honour, Prince vowed not to tone things down and to meet the PMRC head on, so to speak. Ironically, in this, Prince was something of a pioneer. Back in 1985, he was virtually the only black artist to incur the blue-rinsed wrath of the PMRC. In the 21st century, however, 'explicit warning' labels have become almost exclusively a black phenomenon.

Another aspect of the success of the *Purple Rain* album– movie project was that it projected an image of Prince as human – with real friends. Not just some stone-faced musical Svengali who didn't need or want anyone else to help him. But a real guy in a real band. With the arrival of Wendy Melvoin, Lisa Coleman's real-life partner, there was also a sense of Prince as an empowering, life-affirming figure. Yes, Wendy was dressed onstage in stockings and suspenders. But Prince was the one really showing flesh.

'We were absolute musical equals in the sense that Prince respected us, and allowed us to contribute to the music without any interference,' said Melvoin in 1997. 'I think the secret to our working relationship was that we were very non-possessive about our ideas, as opposed to some other people that have worked with him. We didn't hoard stuff, and were more than willing to give him what he needed. Men are very competitive, so if somebody came up with a melody line, they would want credit for it.' In fact, the girls' influence on Prince extended far beyond simple chord progressions or ideas for harmonies. Relaxing at home they introduced Prince to the music of Stravinsky, Vaughan Williams, Scarlatti – and, in particular, Ravel, whose *Bolero* Prince became besotted with.

Wendy's arrival introduced a new dynamic into the band, as Lisa Coleman's live-in partner. 'Lisa and I had known each other since we were two years old,' Wendy recalled in an interview with *Out* magazine in 2009. 'Our families grew up together. We had bands together. We went to the same schools together, the whole thing. And then during those pivotal teenage years, we spent a few years apart. I turned 16 and fell in love with her.' They had been a 'full-blown couple' since 1981. To add to the familial love tangle, Prince also now began dating Wendy's twin sister, Susannah Melvoin – another talented musician.

Although Prince was always extremely demanding – calling up band members in the middle of the night to come and record or simply jam on some ideas, always expecting everyone to be at his beck and call, on the road or off – for Wendy he was simply 'brilliant, enigmatic, strong, aesthetically pleasing, sensual, intellectual, philosophical, more than musical. If he feels comfortable with you he'll crack you up.'

It was plain even to the most casual audience member though that Prince felt equally strongly about his musical relationship with the girls in his band, probably more so than with any male member, past or present. He would openly refer to them as his 'right hand' and came to trust their musical judgement so much that he felt relaxed enough to allow them to do their own work on the songs in the studio. 'Our involvement was obviously important but you have to remember that when he hires you, he hires you as part of a band, not as a solo artist. Whatever Prince saw as the direction to go in, we'd follow him and hopefully be able to contribute something as it evolved.'

How comfortable were they both though with the way Prince expected them to dress onstage, particularly Wendy, who didn't always look entirely at ease in her stockings and suspenders?

'He was incredibly conscious of it,' Wendy said in *Out*. 'He was so androgynous. He didn't care . . . That guy wanted fans. So anyway he could get them . . . appealed to him. The Sly & the Family Stone mentality, that whole black/white/freaky thing on stage appealed to him.'

Lisa pointed out that she and Wendy were never expected to act onstage the way Prince's backing singers or dancers would sometimes be. As far as Lisa was concerned, the audience knew she and Wendy were a couple – and Prince was aware of that too. 'We were the gay girls in the band. It was very calculated.' She went on, 'It was validating. It was just, "Here you go. This is the name of the story and this is what it looks like." And it was all the more reason why we didn't feel as though we had to talk about it.'

Wendy recalled she and Lisa getting a lot of letters from teenage girls that had seen them at a Prince show. 'You could tell in some of the writing that they were little young lesbians and their parents were freaked. And I would write back and just be like, "Just go for it. Live it. You'll work it out."' They even got special attention from straight girls, who would say, 'You're the only gay girls who I'd wanna screw.'

Prince, as always, revelled in the ambiguity, the questioning, the knowing and not knowing. The sexual mystique and rule breaking. Prince may have come across often as a growling three-star general, demanding total loyalty and supreme commitment from his group. But at heart he was the most promiscuous man you could ever meet. He didn't just like one genre of music, he liked them *all*. And he didn't ever want his music or his band to be perceived in just one kind of way. For him, having Wendy and Lisa figuring so prominently in The Revolution was a supremely revolutionary act. It made his music – who he really was – seem just a little bit more special.

Which was another reason why he liked working with his other acts too. At the same time as recording *Purple Rain*, Prince had also co-written, played and produced – under the pseudonym once again of Jamie Starr – a new album for The Time, *Ice Cream Castle*, with several of its tracks also featured in the *Purple Rain* movie. 'That whole period was like boot camp,' Matt Fink would later recall. 'He knew this was a major deal for him, and he certainly felt a lot of pressure to pull it off. He made it very clear to all of us that we had to be disciplined in our work and dedicated to what we were doing. He just worked non-stop; he never slept.'

The *Purple Rain* world tour, which opened in Detroit, on 4 November 1984, was, by common agreement of all who were part of it, not least its star, who summed it up in one word, 'Crazy.' Or as Matt Fink put it: 'That was the closest thing to The Beatles that I've ever experienced. It was just insanity.'

I was there at the Joe Louis Arena for the opening of the tour – a 20,000-capacity riverside arena thronged by masses of people determined that this would be the night they went crazy. Ticket touts were flogging eagle-nest seats for $100 a pop – ten times their face value. You'd never have known America was just 48 hours away from a presidential election. Who cares about Reagan versus Mondale when the biggest tour of the year is in town? Over 300 journalists and photographers had flown in from all corners of the globe. Some of us were syphoned off into our own 'area', that is, a large room with nothing to eat or drink, which people immediately started leaving. In the real VIP section could be glimpsed Apollonia, Jerome Benton and various Warner's execs, along with an unfeasibly high number of the most beautiful women in the world.

Inside the arena the crowd was mainly white. But it looked like most groups were represented: boys and girls; women and men; all dressed according to whatever cultural uniform they feel they most belonged to. And a lot of dazed and confused in between. Shes and hes in high heels and purple lipstick and thin, wispy blondes in purple-dyed hair. More posing and pouting than at a fashion parade. The place was also swarming in security. Hundreds of cops beefed up by even more po-faced types in tour shirts and special badges.

The show was suitably, overwhelmingly spectacular. Huge explosions of pyro, Prince in purple jacket sliding down a fireman's pole onto the stage as the band threw their weight behind 'Let's Go Crazy'. The audience hypnotized as waterfalls of purple confetti tumbled from the rafters. Everybody's favourite Prince song seemed to be included, from obvious hits like 'When Doves Cry', 'Little Red Corvette' and '1999' to deeper cuts like 'God' and 'Father's Song', and some instrumental passages no one yet knew the names of. There were also a bewildering array of costume changes, black leather one minute, white silks the next, the band plugging the disappearances by jamming out songs to twice their recorded length. None of it, miraculously, seemed laboured, it was simply too much fun for that. There was too much to look at and enjoy as well as listen to. Wendy and Lisa, in particular, were starting to look like major stars in their own right.

When the show was over there was a sense of deflation. I knew there would be other great concerts I would go to in my life. Just not that many, if at all, as good as this one had been. As the weeks went by it became clear from other eyewitness accounts that Prince was refreshing the set list every night. I was particularly intrigued to learn he was occasionally adding his version of Joni Mitchell's 'A Case of You' into the show, pouring his heart out at the piano, the keys tinkling gently like wine. This, it was already clear, was an imperial phase for Prince. His only real competition was now himself. Unlike the other regents of Eighties pop and rock – Springsteen, Michael Jackson, Madonna, Dire Straits – Prince really could do it all.

Increasingly, he was being cited as the main 'rival' to Michael Jackson's chart supremacy. Prince didn't deny it at the time, secretly flattered by the comparison. In his heart, though, he understood that the only meaningful similarity between the two was that they had embraced the video age like no other artist: Michael with his game changing, 13-minute 'Thriller' video; Prince, with his movie, *Purple Rain*.

'Michael and I both came along at a time when there was nothing,' Prince would later reason. 'MTV didn't have anyone who was visual. A lot of people made great records, but dressed like they were going to the supermarket.'

Fame on such a global scale can quickly become its own kind of trap, though, as Michael Jackson had known for most of his life – and Prince was only now discovering. The *Purple Rain* world tour had been devised to both promote the movie and the album it was named after, but also to prove once and for all the validity of Prince's demand to be taken seriously. Not just the cute protégé who could play every instrument, or the vainglorious shill in the thongs and long raincoat, nor even the MTV-friendly hit-maker of *1999*. The whole point of *Purple Rain* and its victory lap tour was to demonstrate that Prince was a consummate artist. Successful, yes, but, most of all, *important*. In the same way James Brown and Sly & The Family Stone had been for him. Like the Stones, with hit after hit, but a cultural significance beyond their music even. Or a black David Bowie, daisy-hopping genres and different media, keeping the whole world guessing.

Instead, he found himself locked into a show that increasingly depended for its impact on basically replicating the music-performance scenes from the movie. It took him years to finally process what had happened to him on that tour. Until, finally, speaking to the *Guardian* in 2011, he confessed: 'Purple Rain was 100 shows, and around the 75th, I went crazy, and here's why. They didn't want to see anything but the movie. If you didn't play every song, you were in trouble. After 75 [shows] you don't know where you are – somebody had to drag me to the stage. "I'm not going!" "Yes you are!" It was bloody back then. I won't say why but there was blood on me. They were the longest shows because you knew what was going to happen.'

Maybe so. But that didn't stop Prince the perfectionist running 'the tour like it was the Marines', according to the sax player Eric Leeds. The tour also travelled with a mobile recording truck, so that Prince could record and listen back to every single performance. Soundchecks were also recorded. As were after-show jams. 'That tour really closed the book in that chapter of his life, though,' reckoned Leeds. 'After that things started to open up a little. He had accomplished what he wanted to accomplish and that gave him the opportunity to grow.'

The *Purple Rain* album eventually boasted five hit singles, and would go on to win two Grammys for its creator. When he turned up to receive his Oscar for the film score, at the Dorothy Chandler Pavilion in LA, in March 1985, he was dressed in what looked like a luxuriant pair of purple pyjamas. 'Prince is bringing back the old days of Hollywood,' quipped The Revolution's drummer, Bobby Z. If so, Prince seemed to understand this to mean he should now behave as inscrutably as a Zen master, refusing to wave to his pleading fans as he left the Oscars, or even to smile and look pleased with himself.

Maybe the straitjacket of doing 100 almost identical shows really had driven him temporarily mad, but suddenly Prince seemed to be cultivating a new, more austere image for himself. In recent weeks he'd been reported as visiting a New York disco, where he stood in a circle of bodyguards and danced by himself. In January 1985, when Prince had been easily the runaway winner at the annual American Music Awards, trouncing *Thriller* along the way, every time he walked to the podium to receive yet another award he did so in the mighty shadow of his giant bodyguard, Big Chick.

It was also noted that he had his right eye covered by a be-jewelled purple headscarf. Receiving the award from the Beach Boys for Favorite Black Single – 'When Doves Cry' – Prince issued a terse 'thank you very much' and left the stage.

When he went up to receive the prize for Favorite Black

Album, *Purple Rain*, again beating *Thriller* along the way, Prince walked up with the rest of The Revolution, and instructed Wendy to give the speech: 'On behalf of Prince and The Revolution,' she began, all smiles, 'we would like to thank you for believing and sharing with us what we've been able to create for everybody on vinyl. We'd also like to tell you that we believe in the spirit and we thank you for believing too.' She then held up the award. 'Thank you for this award,' she said. Then walked off, leading the rest of the band – and Prince – with her.

Accepting his third award of the night – for Favourite Pop Album, *Purple Rain* beating *Thriller* a third time – from, of all people, Vanity, Prince, smiling this time, finally managed to conjure up a few words: 'I . . . um . . . for all of us . . . life is death . . . without adventure. And . . . adventure only comes to those who are willing to . . . be daring and take chances.' Another pause. 'I just wanna thank, first of all, God . . . all of the American public . . . my band: Wendy, Lisa, Matt, Mark and Bobby. And, ah, all the staff at Warner Brothers. Dick Clark who could not be here tonight. I don't know . . . I'm very thankful to be here, very thankful to all of you.' Then he blew a kiss and waved. 'Goodnight.'

The screams were deafening. But not everyone was as ecstatic as the fans. Lionel Ritchie, hosting the show, was completely at a loss what to say after every visitation to the podium by the Purple Prince. 'Wow . . . Outrageous! Outrageous!' Not knowing if it was a joke or even if he was supposed to be in on the joke or perhaps the butt of it.

Even other rock stars were now beginning to publicly question his antics. Keith Richards was quoted as saying, 'He's got a problem with his attitude . . . He's a prince who thinks he's a king already.' Daryl Hall, then one of the biggest stars in the world, with Hall & Oates, was said to have sneered, 'He ain't exactly what you'd call a nice guy.' And Night Ranger, who sat in front of Prince at the American Music Awards, claimed they were 'told in no uncertain terms not to talk to him or even acknowledge his presence'.

There was no doubting the sincerity or heart in the live performance Prince & The Revolution gave that night of 'Purple Rain', when he almost appeared to be crying at different moments. Before bringing the whole room to its emotional knees with an absolute fireball of a guitar solo. Striding around the stage in a magnificent ankle-length emerald coat. Truly, that old cliché about letting the music do the talking had never been more apt.

More difficult to understand, at the time, was Prince's refusal to take part in the star-studded recording of America's official contribution to Bob Geldof's Band Aid charity, the 'USA for Africa' single, 'We Are the World', co-written by Michael Jackson and Lionel Ritchie and produced by Quincy Jones. Sessions were even booked in a nearby Hollywood studio for after the American Music Awards show, to ensure as many huge name stars as possible could be there, including Bob Dylan, Ray Charles, Bruce Springsteen, Tina Turner, Diana Ross, Stevie Wonder and Paul Simon. But not Prince. He reportedly went out on the town instead. When asked by one intrepid on-the-spot news reporter why he wasn't participating in what was expected to be one of the biggest fundraising singles of all time (it eventually sold more than 20 million copies worldwide), Prince just deadpanned: 'I don't like to talk too much. I like to act.'

In the event, he did donate a song to the subsequent *We Are the World* album, the lyrically pious but musically, it has to be admitted, somewhat throwaway '4 the Tears in Your Eyes'. He did not, however, agree to perform at the Philadelphia end of the globe-straddling Live Aid concert on 13 July that year.

By then Prince was already onto new things. Things to do with feeding his mind. Musical tripping. You'd see . . .

7

Pop Life

After the final show of the *Purple Rain* tour, at Miami's Orange Bowl – renamed for the night the Purple Bowl – in April 1985, Prince announced what he described as his 'retirement from live performance'. He was going off to 'find the ladder', he announced. By now not much Prince did in public surprised his fans. But this came as a shock. No more shows from the world's greatest showman? And what was this 'ladder' he spoke of? Jacob's ladder? A ladder in Sheila E's stockings? What?

All would be revealed in good – or bad – time: whatever came first. Prince was now thinking of other things. Not least, his next album. It had to be more than just another album, though, he decided. It had to be a musical and artistic statement entirely separate to the one he'd just made with *Purple Rain*.

Had Prince been just like the others – and that includes Madonna, Springsteen and Michael Jackson – his follow-up to *Purple Rain* would have been exactly that. A follow-up. Along with the movie sequel: *Purple Rain II*.

Instead, because he was Prince and he could do whatever he liked, damn the torpedoes, he went in a completely unexpected direction. And he did it fast. The next Prince album, an illicit confection of pop psychedelia, feathered funk and deeply soulful, jazzy ballads titled *Around the World in a Day*, was released just ten months after *Purple Rain*. Compared to Madonna, who took two years to release her follow-up to *Like a Virgin*, or Springsteen, who took three years to follow *Born In The USA*, or the ubiquitous Michael Jackson, who took *five years* to build a plausible sequel to *Thriller*, Prince was moving at light speed.

The critics couldn't keep up, huffing and puffing as they tried to understand why Prince had strayed so far from the *Purple Rain* template. 'Prince's musical fusions smack more of a dead-end desperation than convincing experiment with form,' sneered the *NME*. 'Let's not take Prince's psychedelic trappings too seriously,' urged *Rolling Stone*. Only the *New York Times* got it in one, describing *Around the World in a Day* as 'ambitious, complex and stylistically diverse but at the same time a unified whole – a "concept album" in the tradition of such 60s classics as the Beatles' *Sgt. Pepper's Lonely Hearts Club Band*.'

Indeed, the two albums had much in common, not least their Pop Art covers, though Prince's childlike drawing was perhaps more redolent of *Yellow Submarine*. The music though was all swirling incense and one-with-the-universe pop mysticism, and no less refreshing for that at a time, the mid-Eighties, when Ronald Reagan and Margaret Thatcher were leading the world into a tightly Filofaxed money-driven monoculture that didn't have time to stop and smell the roses.

There were other comparisons with The Beatles of the mid-Sixties. Having announced at the start of 1985 that he was 'retiring' from live performance in order to go in search of 'the ladder', just as The Beatles had 'retired' from concert-giving when they realised the more complex music they were now

making in the studio could not possibly be reproduced satis-
factorily in live performance, Prince seemed to have seized the
moment to make his most musically unexpected album yet.

The album begins with the panoramic title track, the music
drifting in like dawn mist at the start of what looks like it's
going to be a lovely day, all pan pipes and tambourines, Prince
beseeching the world to 'Open your heart, open your minds . . .'
There are vaguely Asian-sounding strings, light gospel voices
and a drifting rhythm that even when Prince opens his throat
and lets go still evokes a sense of bucolic ease and wonder. One
of two tracks on the album co-written with Prince's father,
John, it's another signal of the album's attempt to heal past
wounds, and bring one another together, for ever – and all that
stuff.

The other eight tracks follow suit, more or less. Recorded on
the move across four different studios in Minneapolis and LA,
the various singles give a sense of travelling light, beginning
with 'Paisley Park', actually recorded prior to the material on
Purple Rain, an indication that this was all part of some larger
concept Prince already had. Step one, seduce the straights
with a yummy pop hit ('Wanna Be'), step two, give them some
freaky-deaky to shake them bozos up (*Dirty Mind*), step three,
combine the two and add some Flash Gordon sparks (*Controversy* and *1999*), step four, blow what's left of their tiny minds
with the most anthemic arena-rock album since Led Zeppelin
left the planet (*Purple Rain*).

And now this – Prince's version of getting back to the garden.
Hence the song 'Paisley Park' and its euphoric nod to late-Six-
ties pop whimsy. One of four singles eventually lifted from the
album and, like the gloriously catchy 'Raspberry Beret' and its
glamorous twin, 'Pop Life', it was purposely aimed at bringing

a kind of bedazzled joy to the world's charts. This was Prince singing at home in the bathtub, only much, much better than anyone else did it.

The album still had its edges, but even then there was an almost cartoonish aspect to the album's rougher moments. Like 'America', a fast-paced neo-protest song about an American everykid named Jimmy Nothing, who 'never went 2 school' because it wasn't cool. And because he found so little about his country to be proud of, 'Now Jimmy lives on a mushroom cloud.' Heard for the first time in 1965 it might have had some dramatic impact. Viewed through the prism of 1985, however, it was hard to believe Prince could sing it with a straight face.

But then there were far more self-consciously meaningful moments than that on *Around the World*, some of them very beautiful indeed, like the jazzy piano ballad 'Condition of the Heart', where Prince emotes like Marvin Gaye. Some are so laden down with their own self-importance they fail to make it off the runway – like 'The Ladder', co-written with his father, referencing Prince's comment about going off to find the ladder; it's a slow, luxuriantly produced epic about 'salvation of the soul' that seems to take for ever to get anywhere, then, just as the end is in sight, quickly fades from view.

The only real moment when Prince cuts loose as he did on *Purple Rain* is on the album closer and at eight minutes-plus its longest track, 'Temptation', where the old devil-horned love-demon returns to rock you up until you start to cry, replete with nasty guitar, groin-thrusting drums and a low-growling voice that only comes out at night, before leading the album to the exit sign in the same kind of stoned, lost-focus haze it had begun in. Far out, man.

As if to emphasise how much he saw the album working

as a whole, only fully appreciated when listened to like you read a book, by taking it in through start, middle and ending, Prince refused to release any of the spangled tracks earmarked as singles until the album had already been out and sitting at No. 1 in the charts for two months. But when they did, both 'Raspberry Beret' and 'Pop Life' followed each other into the Top 10.

If not everybody was quite prepared to get fully onboard with the new album, Prince had at least confounded critical expectation again and piqued the public interest. Interview requests poured in from all over the world but Prince shrewdly only agreed to one, from *Rolling Stone*, still in the Eighties the pre-eminent music publication.

Questioned on how much he'd been influenced by *Sgt Pepper*-era Beatles, he shrugged off the comparison. 'They were great for what they did, but I don't know how that would hang today.' He was happy to embrace the description of *Around the World* being deliberately psychedelic, he said, 'because that was the only period in recent history that delivered songs and colours'. Mainly, though, he refused to take seriously the views of critics whom he characterised as 'some mama-jamma wearing glasses and an alligator shirt behind a typewriter'. The message of all his songs now, he insisted, was that 'Nobody's perfect, but they can be. We may never reach that, but it's better to strive than not.'

It's easier now to look back and see *Around the World* as the spiritual progenitor of a whole raft of psychedelic-soul boys from Terence Trent D'Arby, who burst onto the world with his multi-platinum debut, *Introducing the Hardline According to Terence Trent D'Arby*, released two years after *Around the World*, but clearly musically in thrall to it, to Lenny Kravitz, whose own determinedly groovy debut, *Let Love In*, came just two years after that.

Warner's may have been ashen-faced at the prospect of not cashing in more directly on the commercial tumult of *Purple Rain*, but in retrospect *Around the World* was exactly the right move for Prince. Sticking rigidly to the hit-making template would have brought ever-diminishing returns, in terms of credibility and influence. A thoroughly well-versed music historian, Prince understood how important it was for David Bowie to 'retire' Ziggy Stardust before the story got old, how The Beatles had achieved pop immortality by always staying one step ahead. How Stevie Wonder went from chart-topper to mind-maker with a string of albums in the Seventies no one saw coming. 'They didn't know they needed it until they knew they needed it,' as Frank Zappa, the doyen of never giving people what they think they want, once said.

Prince refused to be trapped on the by-the-numbers rock'n'roll merry-go-round. If he'd toured in the summer of 1985 it would most likely have been the highest-grossing tour of the year. Instead he sat down to work on another film project. Again, something so far removed from *Purple Rain* it was like starting all over again. It was called *Under the Cherry Moon*.

Released on 4 July 1986, *Under the Cherry Moon* was ostensibly the story of an American gigolo, Christopher Tracy, played by Prince, and his partner in crime, Tricky, played by The Time's Jerome Benton, who live their lives successfully swindling a series of gullible but always beautiful French women out of their fortunes. Tracy meets his match, though, in the heiress Mary Sharon, played by Kristen Scott Thomas in her first big screen role, and her not-so-easily-fooled father,

Isaac, played by the impressively hostile Steven Berkoff. In short, the sort of cinematic folderol that has been the commercial mainstay of most Hollywood musicals since the dawn of celluloid – and no reason, on paper, why it shouldn't have worked again here.

Only it didn't. Written by Becky Johnston, whose 1991 screenplay for *Prince of Tides* would bring her an Academy Award nomination, the story is not so much at fault as the amateurish acting of Prince and Benton, and, it has to be said, the less than expert direction from Prince himself. (Mary Lambert, who had directed award-winning videos for Madonna and Janet Jackson had originally been in place to direct but departed after one run-in too many with Prince.) Whereas the somewhat two-dimensional character Prince played in *Purple Rain* fitted easily into a setting so openly built on musical and sexual fantasy, *Under the Cherry Moon* demanded much more convincing performances than the wafer-thin turns provided.

As a musical, it couldn't help but captivate Prince's most staunch fans. But as a mainstream Hollywood movie it simply never broke through that fan-only barrier. Of course, the film critics, who'd been baffled by the gargantuan success of *Purple Rain*, had a field day, highlighted by the fact that *Under the Cherry Moon* won multiple awards at the 7th Golden Raspberry Awards: Worst Picture (tied with *Howard the Duck*), Worst Actor and Worst Director (both for Prince), Worst Supporting Actor (Jerome Benton) and even Worst Original Song (for 'Love or Money', written and sung by Prince). Kristen Scott Thomas also received the award for Worst New Star, while Becky Johnston picked up Worst Screenplay. As a result, despite a huge promotional push, including a premier beamed live on MTV, the movie was a flop, barely making $10 million in box office revenue, whereas *Purple Rain* had made nearly 20 times that.

So much of the criticism though was clearly payback for Prince's earlier huge success. Looked at now, one can only applaud the sheer audacity Prince displayed in both starring in and directing a movie he so clearly intended to go so much further than *Purple Rain* had been able to. It was shot in black and white, but the movie buffs neglected to note how much of the movie is obviously influenced by the auteurs of European cinema, not least Antonioni. The kind of movie the words 'cult classic' were invented to describe, *Under the Cherry Moon* was hugely misunderstood and far too easily ridiculed. Try to imagine a contemporary 21st-century music artist like, say, Kanye West or Justin Timberlake undertaking a similar project – impossible!

The album that was released in accompaniment to the film, but specifically not marketed as a soundtrack album per se – *Parade* – also received a mixed reception, and for somewhat similar reasons. Namely, that it veered too far from what Prince was supposed to be good at. Not enough blistering guitar, said some. Not enough bad-ass funk, said many more. Generally, just not enough purple seemed to be what most were saying. Or at least not as the critics had come to expect it. Which was, of course, the point.

Again, in retrospect, this seems entirely out of whack with how the album is perceived now, 30 years on. Example: the first single from the album, one of the most memorable and classically wonderful – not to mention most successful – hits in the Prince canon, 'Kiss'. Prince's first No. 1 American smash hit since 'Let's Go Crazy' two years before, 'Kiss' had originally been a short acoustic demo, barely a minute long, which he had given to Mazarati, the side-band formed by The

Revolution's bassist, Mark Brown. But when Brown and his cohorts worked the demo up into a stripped-down pop-funk hit in the making, Prince was so awestruck he took the song back, adding his own Smokey Robinson-style falsetto to it and that infectious guitar jingle-jangle which became the song's musical calling-card – along with that pouting little x Prince gives it just before the payoff line of the new chorus he also added. When the song was conjoined with the skin-tingling video of a shirtless Prince dancing with veiled dancer Monique Manning, wearing black lingerie and aviator sunglasses – natch – while Wendy Melvoin, pretty in tasselled pink, sits on a stool looking far too cool as she teases out the guitar blushes, it brought Prince back into the living rooms of every country in the world. It also contained some of the most quotable lines in Eighties music: 'Act your age not your shoe size'. 'You don't have to watch *Dynasty* to have an attitude'. And, of course, 'women not girls', ruling Prince's world. Fabulous.

A last-minute addition to *Parade*, 'Kiss', you might say, made the album worth the price of admission alone. In fact, it was merely the icing on the cake. If *Parade* was considered a patchy album it was still on a higher level to virtually anything else released in 1986, in terms of originality and style. As well as the sumptuous 'Kiss' there were the slinky 'Girls and Boys', which would slide on its knees all the way into the UK Top 10 in the late summer; the brilliantly strutting 'New Position', with its dancing kettle drums and cheeky vocals; and the wonderfully kitsch 'Do U Lie?' Best of all there was 'Mountains', the entirely different follow-up to 'Kiss' as a single that may just be the best song on the album. Co-written with Wendy and Lisa, this was Prince again reaching for new goals – the kind of anthem that would have worked for U2 or Madonna, but in Prince's hands it became an experience as elevated as any to be found in late-Eighties rock.

'Prince would send us masters in LA, and we would work out the arrangements or whatever else, and then send it back to him,' recalled Lisa. 'Often, they would just be skeletons of songs, like [*Parade*'s] "Christopher Tracy's Parade", which was originally called "Little Wendy's Parade". He never second guessed any of the work we did for him.' Prince also later named the ethereal sound of the Cocteau Twins' 1984 album *Treasure* as another important influence on the sound of *Parade*, proving once again just how far and wide his listening habits went – and how uninhibited he was about incorporating all spheres of artistic influence into his work.

Not all of this was picked up on by the reviewers of the day, many of whom were now enjoying getting their hooks into the upstart maverick who no longer granted interviews or played the game of loaded dice they preferred to indulge in. The *NME* once again excelled in this regard, regarding 'Kiss' as little more than a 'throwback' to *Dirty Mind*-era Prince, before concluding by posing the question: 'Is it possible, or even advisable, to take Prince seriously? Do I have to watch *Dynasty* to have an attitude? I find this record laboured and trite and self-satisfied and won't be listening to it again.' *Rolling Stone* came to the rescue this time though, when it concluded its review thus: 'Having gathered enough laurels on which to rest comfortably for ever more, Prince wants to have some fun with music, or as he puts it, to "go fishing in the river, the river of life." What better time for a new baptism?'

Prince, though, was no longer dependent on reviews. He was far too busy living the life – warts and all. One of the songs he wrote for *Under the Cherry Moon* that didn't make it on

Parade – 'Old Friends 4 Sale' – was said to contain barely concealed references to the firing of Jimmy Jam and Terry Lewis, both of whom had gone on to great success as the production team behind Janet Jackson. There were also veiled references to Big Chick Huntsberry, who had more recently been fired after it was alleged that Chick had sold a gossip story about Prince to a tabloid, in order to support a cocaine habit.

The headline in the 7 May 1985 edition of the *National Enquirer* read: 'the real Prince – he's trapped in a bizarre secret world of terror'. In the story Chick was quoted as saying that Prince lived as an eccentric recluse, describing some Marilyn Monroe posters he owned as a 'shrine', and painting a picture of Prince's home as being guarded by armed bodyguards and even a food-taster. The general gist was that Prince was paranoid for his life, surrounded by flunkies and groupies.

Asked to comment by *Rolling Stone*, Prince batted the story away at first. 'I never believe anything in the *Enquirer*,' he told them. But the more he thought about it, the angrier he became. And although 'Old Friends 4 Sale' was eventually re-recorded in 1991, with less personal lyrics, and eventually released on a compilation of previously unreleased material in 1996, Prince never forgave Chick for betraying him.

As usual, Prince was also becoming entangled yet again in his more personal relationships. While he was in Monte Carlo filming *Cherry Moon*, his latest love, Sheila E, was also starring in the cult hip-hop movie *Krush Groove*, co-starring the 21-year-old heart-throb Blair Underwood in his movie debut, a biopic about the early, harum-scarum days of Def Jam Records. The shooting of the movie was constantly interrupted by the presence of various rap stars, real and fictitious. Unused to this kind of scene, Sheila would phone Prince and complain of being frightened. Prince, meanwhile, was adamant he didn't want his girl shooting the nude scenes the script called for. But Sheila had no choice. In her 2014 memoir *The Beat of My Own Drum*, she wrote how she ended up having a few drinks for Dutch courage before allowing 'Blair to suck on my neck'.

But if Prince was put out by this, he consoled himself with the knowledge that there was always a beautiful woman somewhere on hand to turn to. Many of them famous, too. Indeed, the mid-Eighties found the Purple Prince enjoying the company of several well-known women, including Madonna, Kim Basinger and, in 1985, Susanna Hoffs. Hoffs was the singer of a then little-known all-female pop-punk outfit from LA called The Bangles, whose career Prince singlehandedly transformed when he gave them a song he'd originally written for Apollonia, titled 'Manic Mondays'. Released early in 1986, 'Manic Mondays' (with Prince credited as writer under the pseudonym of 'Christopher') reached No. 2 in both Britain and America and turned The Bangles into the best-known female group in the world – though by then Prince's own personal relationship with Susanna had officially 'moved on'.

As Jimmy Jam would observe, 'He definitely loved the ladies, and he had impeccable taste in women.' The women that Prince escorted around town would be so unbelievably beautiful, said Jam, 'You think to yourself, "Of course that's Prince's girl. Of course."'

Never one to shy from changing his mind, Prince also announced a new world tour – to begin at First Avenue in Minneapolis, almost exactly a year after announcing he would never tour again, a six-month jaunt around the world that would include two sold-out nights at Madison Square Garden in New York and three more sold-out nights at Wembley Arena in London. The tour was full of pleasing contrasts and firsts, from playing a show in upstate New York transmitted via satellite to 60,000 people in the audience and millions of TV viewers at home, to a surprise show at a tiny club in Boston.

Most of the shows were joyous occasions. The incredible final night at Wembley, which I was there for, including the not really very secret after-show 'jam' at a club in London, proved how easily Prince was able to transform the biggest venue into what seemed like just another extension of First Avenue. 'For us the greatest moment was at Wembley, when we were playing onstage with Ron Wood and Eric Clapton,' laughed Wendy. 'That was like fantasy come true.'

Yet what nobody realised until it was too late, not even the band, was that these really would be the last shows Prince would perform with The Revolution. Most poignantly, the last that would include both Wendy and Lisa. 'The last gig we played with The Revolution [was] at the Yokohama Stadium [in Japan],' recalled Wendy. 'We knew it'd be the last time for a while that we'd be onstage together. He broke all his *Purple Rain* guitars during "Purple Rain" and walked off. "Sometimes It Snows in April" was the encore and we all felt this incredible power onstage. It was almost heartbreaking.'

It would be years, though, before either Wendy or Lisa could really begin to process the incredible journey Prince had taken them on during those helter-skelter years. In fact, it wasn't until after they ceased to be a couple, in 2002, that they felt they could even talk about it in public. Having continued as best friends, they had managed to also continue working together as musicians.

When *Out* magazine asked, in 2009, if either of them now felt they had been exploited 'to assert Prince's heterosexuality', they both admitted they felt differently about the whole thing. Lisa wasn't sure their onstage performances were about Prince's heterosexuality as much as they were about her and Wendy's sexuality. Wendy, who had been the one in the stockings and suspenders in the *Purple Rain* movie, and had more of the interaction on stage with Prince during their years of touring, immediately answered yes, though.

She elaborated: 'Towards the very end of our relationship together as a working triumvirate, yes. It felt more like he had used up all he needed from us and he was going on to something else. [But] as a lesbian couple, we weren't playing that sexuality with him specifically, and I think that maybe he needed more of that playfulness, and that probably came from him wanting to exploit his heterosexual side more. Maybe it was unconscious, but yeah, for sure.'

Whatever its eventual outcome, by the time the *Parade* world tour had concluded with those two sold-out shows at the 30,000-capacity Yokohama Stadium, in September 1986, Prince was now, indisputably, the definitive pop icon of the Eighties. A nothing-he-can't-do one-man band who danced as brilliantly as he played guitars, sang as beautifully as he produced records, a seemingly effortless hit-maker for both himself and a score of other artists, a true maverick at a time of great conformity whose tours were now the greatest spectacles in the world of contemporary music. And so damn love-sexy it made grown men weep with envy and ladies of a certain age go weak at their matrimonial bonds.

Of all his many talents, perhaps his greatest feat was finding a way to meld the past with the future, to create a different kind of now – one of infinite possibilities. People talked of his resemblance to Jimi Hendrix when he played that curvaceous white Telecaster, which he would hurl into the audience with that knowing smile that made you realise he'd seen more of the dark stuff than most men even know exists. It was all there on 'Sign o' the Times', the kind of blood-spilled street talk it would be years before any other black artist learned to go the same way.

But then there was his childlike devotion to the kind of soulful pop only fully realised women-not-girls could understand. In songs like 'Kiss' he said things no other guy would have been smart enough to say, the real things potential girlfriends and wives longed to hear. About vulnerability and sincerity and honesty – and the strength that only came from a gently beating heart. In 'Sometimes It Snows in April', it's like Prince is channelling Brian Wilson, alone in the studio while the rest of the Beach Boys remain locked outside wondering why he's so sad.

Then there was his one-on-one relationship with God, a fusion of spirituality and sex unseen since the bewilderingly intoxicated, joyously mournful days (and nights) of Little Richard, Jim Morrison and Marvin Gaye. And a thrilling disregard for colour – outside purple – unseen since Sly Stone mixed black and white with male and female in the Family Stone. For Prince race and sex and God and music were best when all rolled into a two-way street up and down which almost anything could and would happen.

The only plausible rival left to Prince was Michael Jackson, and even the self-styled King of Pop was now convinced that Prince had come along and stolen his lunch money, in music biz parlance. For while *Thriller* had become the biggest-selling album of all time, it was still *Purple Rain* that received the most critical plaudits. And while Jackson was busy having plastic surgery to reconstruct his eyes, his nose, his chin, eventually even turning to chemicals to try and turn his skin white, Prince had done all of that seemingly overnight without changing a damn thing about the way he looked. In short, Michael Jackson was jealous of Prince, as being the only performer left in the contemporary music landscape to rival Jackson's own vaulting ambitions. In a bizarre attempt to cut his only rival down to size, Jackson invited Prince to appear in his 'Bad' video – the part eventually taken by Wesley Snipes. As Prince later explained in an interview with the comedian Chris Rock, 'The first line in that song is, "Your butt is mine", now who gonna sing that to whom? Because you sure ain't singing that to me. And I sure ain't singing that to you.'

The odd thing was how much the two resembled each other – different sides of the same coin, in so many ways: both über-talented light-skinned black men who had become the most successful entertainers in the world. Michael had the edge in terms of sheer sales, but it was Prince who had all the credibility – a fact that Jackson's veteran producer, Quincy Jones, was trying to address, perhaps, when he did something no one else had imagined possible: bringing the two superstars together. Officially, what Quincy said he was hoping for was that some of Prince's can-do attitude would rub off on Michael, whose interplanetary success with *Thriller* had had the opposite effect to Prince and *Purple Rain*: instead of it galvanising him to go bigger and better, Jackson had fallen into a creative funk that Jones was now desperately trying to pull him out of – by any means necessary.

Prince read all this but instinctively felt there was another, ulterior motive to the meeting. That maybe Quincy was hoping Prince might collaborate with Michael. After all, he'd written hit songs for complete unknowns. What might he be able to achieve if he had Michael singing one of his songs. And there was something else. Heavy metal star Eddie van Halen had played the ferocious attention-grabbing guitar on 'Beat It' that single-handedly brought Michael to a new, more album-oriented white rock audience. Might having Prince play his form of universe-baiting guitar on Michael's next album confer a new kind of credibility too? Or how about a duet? Like the one Michael did with Paul McCartney on *Thriller*?

In the event, Prince was way too competitive to allow such things to happen. Why would he want to give his main rival a leg-up when he was so busy building his own empire? In the end it was only Prince's sensibility that Michael Jackson did his best to confer on his next album, *Bad*. He took the clothes – the bad-boy peacock-rock look – and waited for Quincy Jones to toughen up his sound in the studio, which he did.

By the time Jackson's next tour began, in 1987, though, it was clear he could never be mistaken for Prince – and vice-versa. At best, seen in a certain stage light, they might be considered yin-yang. Duelling partners locked into an uneasy symbiosis. Both boys from the Midwest who would never feel entirely embraced by the white establishment their supreme artistry had opened the doors to.

The crucial difference was that Michael Jackson would build himself his own gilded cage out in Los Angeles, name it Neverland and fill it with every strange toy he could think of, while Prince was not prepared to move an inch outside the place he still thought of as home – though he, too, now had designs on building his own highly secure, supremely private work-play-home mansion complex. Only, he named it after one of his own songs – and a recurring dream he'd been having for some time now – Paisley Park.

The difference was symbolic. Michael dealt only in dreams, success came first over everything. Prince was the opposite. He enjoyed the trappings of success too, but only because it allowed him not to try and repeat himself with copycat hits. Prince wanted to go his own way. Even if it meant costing him – money, personal relationships, love. It all came second to the music. The drive. The force.

Jackson might go on to become bigger than The Beatles – safe, cosy, reliable. But Prince would be the Rolling Stones – individualistic, daring, a little too freaky perhaps.

Prince certainly hoped so.

8

Who Knows the Storm

By the end of the world tour in September 1986, it seemed that so many of Prince's dreams had come true he wasn't sure where to go next. 'Kiss' and *Parade* had proved he still owned the charts. The success of The Bangles, whose 'Manic Monday' had only been kept from No. 1 in America by 'Kiss', had been followed by Sheila E's 'Love Bizarre', co-written with Prince, hitting the charts, which in turn was followed by Meli'sa Morgan's version of Prince's 'Do Me Baby' (from *Controversy*) going to No. 1 in the R&B chart.

It wasn't just newcomers or members of Prince's own entourage who were now coming to Prince hoping some of his magic would rub off on them. Stevie Nicks of Fleetwood Mac had enjoyed a solo hit single with 'Stand Back', which Prince had co-written with her. But because Nicks was not signed to Warner's, her label, Modern, decided to leave his name out of the credits. Then there was Chaka Khan's spirited version of 'I Feel for You', from Prince's first album. That had gone to No. 3 in the US and No. 1 in the UK, and melted the Top 10s in every other record-buying country in the world, one of those radio staples they still play today, 30 years later. 'Um, he's different,' Khan would say of Prince. 'But I think that people misread his shyness for something else. He's just introverted and very shy and, um, he's different!'

He certainly was. The year before, Prince had also recently helped rejuvenate Sheena Easton's career by penning her hit 'Sugar Walls', under the pseudonym Alexander Nevermind. 'I walked into the studio and there was no 12 bodyguards, just him,' Easton later recalled. 'He was very quiet and shy.' There was nothing shy about the record though, Easton sweetly beckoning the listener to 'Come spend the night inside my sugar walls'. As a result, it was listed by Tipper Gore's PMRC as one of the 'Filthy Fifteen' songs of the year. Briefly obsessed with the British pop noodle, Prince was credited with giving Easton's prim image a sexy new makeover and she would feature in the following year with him on his 'U Got the Look' hit.

Over the next couple of years Prince would also be cited as the mastermind behind hits for Patti Labelle ('Yo Mister', which he wrote and produced) and Sinéad O'Connor's stunning cover of 'Nothing Compares 2 U'. The stuff that really excited Prince though had little to do with the numbers game of Top 10s or getting songs on the radio. One of the reasons he sponsored so many new acts was because he had to have an outlet for his prodigious talents. Prince never stopped working, couldn't stop writing, never went a day without picking up various instruments and just seeing what would happen. Warner's supported him in this, releasing all the music he made under his various nom-de-plumes, whether it be The Time, Vanity 6, Apollonia, Sheila E, even giving him his own label imprint, Paisley Park, to release his and others' records on.

His latest project, The Family, was born out of the ashes of The Time, who had splintered even before *Purple Rain* was released and turned them into even bigger posthumous stars.

Morris Day, yearning to get out from under Prince's brilliant but domineering influence, had made his dash for stardom as a solo act. That left the guitarist Jesse Johnson as the leader of the band. But when Prince urged him to move the keyboardist Paul Peterson in front of the microphone, Johnson baulked. Jesse saw himself fulfilling that role. So much so, he too soon left The Time, in search of solo success.

Reading the signs, Prince decided to put The Time on ice and instead pulled their remaining members – Peterson, the drummer Jellybean Johnson and backing vocalist, dancer and Day's former comedic foil Jerome Benton – together and proposed a brand-new project to be called The Family. As usual, Prince already had it all worked out. Paul would be the frontman, renamed St Paul, with Johnson and Benton continuing in their usual roles, together with a new member, Wendy Melvoin's twin sister, Susannah, brought in as backing singer – and an element of glamour. The other new member would be the saxophonist Eric Leeds, brother of Prince's longtime tour manager, Alan.

As with all Prince's side projects, he would write all the music, play most of the instruments in the studio, with Paul's and Susannah's voices added to the mix later. The only exceptions to this rule on the album they made together, *The Family Album*, would be the track 'River Run Dry', written by The Revolution's drummer, Bobby Z, and the overdubbed saxophone and flute by Leeds. Released in the latter half of 1985, the album was a blend of high-energy funk, some soft-core jazz-fusion and a couple of so-so ballads, and was only a qualified success, hoovered up by Prince fans but largely ignored by everyone else.

There was, however, one absolutely stand-out track, the

cathedral-like 'Nothing Compares 2 U', written in praise of Susannah Melvoin, whom Prince had reportedly once talked of marriage to, but had now split from, which Prince liked so much that when The Family was disbanded a year later, he decided to start playing it at his own shows. On the *Parade* tour, he had also taken to performing another track from the Family collection, 'Mutiny', which he would stretch out into improvised breaks, adding the chant of 'Dream Factory!' to the chorus, a phrase that would take on greater significance once the tour was over and Prince began to dream big again.

The Family album proved to be the link to yet another, more adventurous side project Prince now turned his attention to over the last months of 1986 – an instrumental jazz-fusion album under the name Madhouse. This time, though, the work would be entirely collaborative, with Prince writing exclusively with Eric Leeds. It marked the first time Prince had loosed the songwriting reins and the result was two superb albums, *8* and *16*, both released in 1987, on the Paisley Park/Warner Bros. imprint. Most remarkable about the music on these records was that the untrained ear would never know Prince was so heavily involved. His appetite for artistic self-aggrandisement apparently satiated – momentarily, at least – Prince buried his identity still further by listing each track as a number: eight tracks on the first album, listed simply as 1, 2, 3 . . . etc., eight tracks on the second, carrying on where the first left off: 9, 10, 11 . . . etc.

There were some low-key Madhouse shows, too, with Prince appearing incognito. Then, in 1987, on the next Prince tour, Madhouse was the opening act, with the band members disguised in baggy cloaks and dark glasses – removed when they returned to play with Prince. There were rumoured to be at least two further Madhouse albums recorded, both of them enigmatically titled *24*, but they were never released.

What was going on? Had Prince gone mad? Actually, no. Quite the opposite, in fact. He merely wanted to make some music that didn't rely on the promotional juggernaut that accompanied his other releases. Sick of being in the company, at least in the public eye, of other Eighties pop goliaths like Michael Jackson and Madonna, Prince was making his bid for a greater glory in his eyes: he wanted to be held in the same esteem as Jimi Hendrix, as Miles Davis, as Mozart. Prince was out to achieve musical godhead and he knew for that you needed to create music that went far beyond the reach of just the Top 10. Music that would speak to the ages.

No surprise then that it should also be at just this moment that he embarked on another semi-secret musical project – with Miles Davis. The two had met by chance at LAX airport, and Prince used the opportunity to let Davis know how much he admired him. Then was blown away to discover just how mutual the feeling was.

As Davis later wrote in his 1989 memoir, *Miles*, the jazz legend had been aware of Prince for some time. 'His shit was the most exciting music I was hearing in 1982,' he wrote, 'so I decided to keep an eye on him . . . Prince got some Marvin Gaye and Jimi Hendrix and Sly in him, also, even Little Richard. He's a mixture of all those guys and Duke Ellington. He reminds me, in a way, of Charlie Chaplin, he and Michael Jackson.' By the time they met in 1986, Davis was convinced that, as he said, 'Prince's music is pointing toward the future.'

Prince could hardly believe his ears. Miles Davis was everything he wanted to be. The most innovative musician of his generation, in classic albums like *Kind of Blue* (1959),

Sketches of Spain (1960) and, more recently, the double master-piece *Bitches Brew* (1970), Davis had single-handedly invented genres of music, from hard bop and modal experimentations, to a musical fusion of American jazz, European classical and some of the earliest excursions into what later became known as world music. Then, in 1970, he'd single-handedly invented jazz-fusion, or what was then known as jazz-rock.

As important as any of this to Prince, though, was the fact that Miles Davis had built a reputation as a supreme badass. The uncooperative black man in a white man's world who frightened the hell out of straitlaced record companies. Who went his own way at all times, was never afraid to speak his mind and didn't care what anybody had to say about it. For Prince, Miles Davis was simply The Man. 'Prince saw in Miles so much of what he thought of himself,' Eric Leeds later re-called. 'The person that goes against the grain, that doesn't allow himself to be controlled by any aspect of the industry for his own artistic vision. And that's very much what Miles saw in Prince. He saw a young version of himself.'

When Miles started talking about 'doing something togeth-er' Prince seized his chance and immediately began writing material for what would be Davis's next album – his first, as it transpired, for Warner's – *Tutu*, released in 1986. Except that when the album arrived there wasn't a single scrap of Prince material there – what had happened?

According to Miles, Prince simply changed his mind at the last minute. Got cold feet, maybe. This wasn't The Bangles or Sheena Easton he was writing for now, this was The Master. A great pity as some of the tracks Prince came up with for Davis later surfaced on various bootlegs and are magnificent, one of the best-known being 'Can I Play with U', a funky, synth-driven workout overlaid with the unmistakable sound of Davis's baleful muted trumpet: like a jazzy James Brown, or a more spaced-out Sly Stone, Prince adding his own beautifully understated but bubbling guitar towards the end.

Miles loved the track and was baffled when Prince asked him not to use it on *Tutu*. Another great set-piece Prince wrote for Davis was called 'Penetration', which Miles loved so much he was still including a scorching version of it in his live show just weeks before he died in 1991 – a great pity as the idea of Miles and Prince finally doing an album together had resurfaced, along with the suggestion they go on tour together. Footage now available on YouTube of a special charity concert for the homeless that Prince gave in 1988 at Paisley Park, to which Davis was invited and appeared onstage gives an enticing glimpse into just what might have been, if the two great black musicians of the late twentieth century had begun to work together in earnest.

As Davis wrote, Prince, just as Miles had done in his younger days, represented 'the music of the people who go out after 10 or 11 at night. . . I think when Prince makes love he hears drums instead of Ravel. For me he can be the new Duke Ellington of our time.'

Newly inspired, Prince now decided to take a further leaf out of the Miles Davis guide to making the music of the gods and allow his band members the freedom finally to express themselves – with some guidance from Prince. But that was all. Given the freedom they'd always begged for, what would they come up with? Prince decided to call the project *Dream Factory*.

This was a musical experiment that had begun towards the end of the *Parade* tour, when Wendy and Lisa were still involved. The fact that the *Dream Factory* album, like the original Miles Davis material, was then dramatically abandoned just as it seemed that it was going to be Prince's next big musical leap into the unknown may also have been a factor in why Prince then decided to dismantle The Revolution entirely, taking Wendy and Lisa with it.

Starting with just two tracks Prince had written – the first, 'The Ballad of Dorothy Parker', about the brilliant American poet and satirist who founded the fabled Algonquin Round Table, was renowned for her razor-sharp epithets such as 'Heterosexuality is not normal, it's just common'; 'You can lead a *horticulture*, but you can't make her think'; and, most pithily when applied to Prince, 'They sicken of the calm who knew the storm.' The idea came to Prince from a dream he had, he said. Lots of songs came that way for Prince. This, though, was a particularly good one: a snappy jazz-inflected romp, like a cat flicking its tail. The other starting point for *Dream Factory* was something he'd written with Susannah Melvoin, 'Starfish and Coffee', an equally sharp groover, catchy as a cold.

The rest of *Dream Factory* though was up to the band. Some of the tracks that came back included only a couple of band members, like the stuff from Wendy and Lisa, other tracks were the whole band working stuff out. At one point, it looked like *Dream Factory* was going to be a 19-track double album, including such titles as 'Sexual Suicide', 'Big Tall Wall', 'All My Dreams' and 'Teacher, Teacher'. Then just as the band believed their dreams of song authorship on a truly collaborative album were finally coming true in a big way, Prince changed his mind, offered no explanation – and cancelled the band.

'He wanted to express himself completely,' Wendy would try to explain it years later. 'We were doing so much work. That's the way I rationalize it now. Prince may have other reasons why he let us go. He's never really talked about that. But we were led to believe that he needed to get back his mojo.' Speaking to *Melody Maker* at the time of the split, Wendy described it magnanimously as 'an abrupt decision, but it felt right . . . being around someone that productive is incredibly inspiring – but even Zen masters need to go off on their own'.

To do that, Prince retreated alone back into the studio and began working on yet another project – to be titled *Camille*: another musical mask for Prince to hide behind but which allowed him to record eight hard-as-nails funk tracks, with speeded-up lead vocals intended to give the impression that *Camille* was neither male nor female, or possibly a little or a lot of both. Bearing little resemblance to anything Prince had released before, the raucous sound of tracks like 'Rebirth of the Flesh' and 'Feel U Up' give the impression of an artist out of control, letting it all hang out, the good, the bad and the sexy, the only truly transcendent moment a gorgeous mid-paced soul ballad called 'If I Was Your Girlfriend', possibly the first 'genderqueer' song in pop history – 20 years before the term was invented.

Within weeks, though, Prince had changed his mind again, opting to roll both *Dream Factory* and *Camille* material into a sprawling triple-album set called *Crystal Ball*. Warner execs were aghast. Utterly supportive of every move Prince had made, from the days when they gave in and let him produce his own first album, to Mo Ostin personally financing what seemed the impossible dream of making his own movie, to the seemingly endless array of side projects and other crazy ideas Prince had, this surely was the last straw. Alarmed at the seemingly cavalier way he'd broken up The Revolution, unsettled by his constant scrapping and revising of his plans, they finally drew the line at releasing a *triple album*.

Prince, to their further astonishment, didn't bat an eyelid. He simply trimmed the track list down and turned the three-disc *Crystal Ball* into a scintillating double set retitled *Sign o' the Times*. And suddenly Prince's career was back on track again.

The first album Prince would record parts of in the sprawling new state-of-the-art studio at the heart of his palatial new home, Paisley Park, the whole album benefits from a new sense of freedom, of renewal. Working via the cutting-edge console Prince had commissioned from the legendary studio guru Frank De Medio – a twin console to the one De Medio had custom-built for Sunset Sound in Los Angeles, where Prince often recorded. But De Medio was a perfectionist and when things seemed to be taking too long, Prince threatened to fire De Medio if the console wasn't finished that week. The console duly installed, Prince could wait no longer and immediately began recording 'The Ballad of Dorothy Parker', even though his in-house engineer, Susan Rogers, hadn't had a chance to even test the new equipment yet.

'As always, he's playing every instrument and I'm just panicking on the inside because something doesn't sound right,' recalled Rogers in 2012. 'It's really dull, there's no high end and I can't wait for this song to be finished because I've got to check it out and see what's going on. Of course, the song is coming out really well and the whole time I'm thinking, "I wish he would just stop", but that's not going to happen,' she laughed. 'At the very end, he gave me my final instructions and he said, "There's something about this console that doesn't sound like the one at Sunset Sound, it's really dull", and then he goes upstairs and goes to bed. I'm thinking, "Hell yeah it's dull, there's no high end at all!" But he conceived of the song in a dream so he didn't mind that at all because it gave it this dream-like quality.'

Prince, normally so fanatical about getting the tiniest detail right, breezed through other tracks while recording in his new Paisley Park studio. 'If I Was Your Girlfriend', the sultry single from the album, came with an accidentally distorted lead vocal you can still hear on the finished track. The louder than hell 'Housequake', one of the most funked-up tracks on the album, was recorded as-live from an improvised late-night jam with The Bangles. And the album's biggest charting single, 'U Got the Look', featuring Sheena Easton, only came about when Easton turned up at Paisley Park unexpectedly one day, curious to check out the new complex, only to be dragged to the mic by Prince.

According to Rogers in an excellent piece by Marc Weingarten, in *MOJO*, in February 1997, 'Sheena came into the studio unannounced one day cos she wanted Prince to produce her next album . . . he didn't feel like socialising, though. "U Got the Look" had gone through a million changes, and he was really struggling with it. He felt this was an important single for him. It was originally a mid-tempo thing, but he had sped it up at the last minute and asked her to sing on it. I think she was a little taken aback by the sexual nature of it at first, but he convinced her to get into it, and it worked perfectly.'

Released in March 1987, in the end *Sign o' the Times* was the best bits of *Dream Factory*, *Camille* and *Crystal Ball*, plus a handful of anthemic Prince showstoppers like 'The Cross', with its haunting guitars, and the brilliant, epically proportioned title track. Although its sales suffered in comparison to his recent hits, *Sign* still reached No. 6 in the US and No. 4 in Britain. But Prince got what he was really looking for in the tsunami of unanimous critical approval that greeted it.

America's pre-eminent music critic, Robert Christgau, not known for overpraising anything, writing in the *Village Voice*, described the album as 'the most gifted pop musician of his generation proving what a motherfucker he is for two discs start to finish'. He said his multi-tracked vocals, 'make Stevie Wonder sound like a struggling ventriloquist', before concluding, no less grandly, that *Sign o' the Times* 'established Prince as the greatest rock and roll musician of the era – as singer-guitarist-hooksmith-beatmaster, he has no peer'. *Rolling Stone*, in a retrospective review, described the album as 'arguably the finest album of the 1980s' and London's arts magazine *Time Out* went even further, ranking it as the greatest album of all time.

The accompanying world tour was Prince's most talked-about since the *Purple Rain* fandango of three years before. He had a new band to show off and a whole new, much more up-scale production to go with it. Wendy and Lisa were no more. Now, though, he had Sheila E on drums: 'By far the best drummer Prince ever had,' according to Eric Leeds. Leeds and Matt Fink were the only holdovers from The Revolution. The rest of the ten-piece band included the guitarist Miko Weaver, bassist Levi Seacer Jr from Sheila E's band and who had had also been part of Prince's Madhouse project, keyboardist Boni Boyer and various backing singers and dancers, led by the beautiful Cat Glover, who'd got her break via the US TV talent show *Star Search*.

In keeping with his new, much freer approach, Prince allowed his show to ebb and flow like never before. Where the *Purple Rain* show had been choreographed to within an inch of its fab-u-lous life, the *Sign o' the Times* show found Prince and his new band stretching out and improvising. Taking their cues from Prince, the band had been rehearsed to allow for over 100 songs, and Prince would decide what they would play on the spot each night. In the manner of James Brown in his imperial heyday, Prince devised a series of hand signals to direct the band. 'If he held up two fingers, you'd hit him two times,' recalled Leeds. 'If he pulled a finger across his throat, you had to end it on the one.'

But while the European dates were a sensation, Prince shelved plans to take the show back on the road in America, where he could no longer be guaranteed to sell out stadiums. Similarly, several planned UK dates were also put on the back-burner. There was talk of the threat of bad weather disrupting the open-air shows, but behind the scenes the real fear was that Prince was simply not going to be able to sell enough tickets to fill the venues. A projected tour of Japan was also shelved.

Instead, the idea was hatched to hurriedly release a concert film of the show, directed by Prince and simply called *Sign o' the Times*. Released in November 1987, the *Sign* movie was exciting, lavish and true to the live show. It couldn't compare with actually being at a live Prince show, though, and its theatre run was brief, its highlights far outweighing its sum parts. Or as *Rolling Stone* put it in its review, '*Sign o' the Times* captures him nicely, but many more people deserve to confront the challenge and the playfulness Prince embodies in the flesh.'

Behind the scenes the tour had also had its share of dramatic moments. Sheila E later recalled the night when Prince turned to her onstage one night halfway through 'Purple Rain' and mouthed the words, 'Marry Me?' Sheila didn't need to be asked twice, though she agreed to Prince's request to keep their engagement secret for the duration of the tour, so as to avoid unnecessary tabloid attention.

In her 2014 memoir *The Beat of My Own Drum*, she wrote: 'He blew me a kiss, turned to the audience, and took the most amazing guitar solo ever. For the rest of that year my relationship with Prince was a dream . . . We were with each other all day and all night, so if he was fooling around on me, he would have had to be quick about it.' But when Prince also began insisting she dress up in more revealing clothes onstage, recalled Sheila, 'I started to feel naked in the wrong way,' she writes.

By the end of tour, instead of looking forward to future marital bliss, Sheila was instead looking at a bill Prince's management had presented her with for all the expenses she racked up on tour: a six-figure sum she had no way of paying. What was worse, she and Prince were no longer even 'a constant' couple.

'I tried to ignore the sadness I felt about not being the only woman in his life, but I learned to deal with it early on,' she revealed.

Prince, though, as ever, had other, more important things on his mind, now the *Sign* tour was over. Taking the band off the road but back into the studio, he began work on what at the time was considered his most controversial album yet – simply titled *The Black Album*. Its origins, it now emerges, lay in a birthday party Prince decided to give Sheila E. According to Susan Rogers, 'Prince wanted to have a big party for [Sheila] in LA, and he wanted to record some mindless party songs for her. The sessions for *Sign* had been so intense, and he just wanted to lay down some mindless jams. Not too much thought went into them.' He simply recorded a hatful of tracks then took

Mayte and the Artist Now Known
As Her Husband . . . (Photoshot).

Symbol unveils his new . . .
Symbol (Photoshot).

Right Prince in 'casual' mode. Replete with the six-inch heels he wore everywhere, even indoors (Getty Images).

Left Prince and Beyoncé, performing together at the Grammy awards show, LA, 2004 (Getty Images).

Below The new, Jehovah-worshipping Prince shows off his iconic 'love symbol' guitar (Alamy).

Right A triumphant Prince at the Super Bowl in 2007. The best Super Bowl halftime show in history, the organisers later proclaim (Getty Images).

Left Prince with second wife, Manuela Testolini, circa 2001 (Rex Features).

Below Prince with Chaka Khan and Stevie Wonder on *Later With Jools Holland* (Getty Images).

A Prince for all times. *Top left*: refusing to
show his face in his 'Slave' days (Photoshot).
Bottom: Prince performing at the MGM
Grand Garden Arena, 2013 (Getty Images).
Above: God, sex, music, it was all one thing
to Prince (Photoshot).

Next page Pure gold, 2015. Prince was
still the most stylish figure in music –
check out the three-lens sunglasses – even
as he battled his demons towards the
end of his life (Getty Images).

an acetate of them to the DJ to play at the party. Dancing to its bawdy, blood-thick grooves, several people at the party urged Prince to make the tracks available to buy. Never shy about putting new products out, Prince announced the next day that he would do exactly that, and that the eight-track acetate would be his next release, titled *The Black Album*. 'Black' as in race: black as in 'X'-rated.

Then, just as the new CD was about to be shipped to retailers, Prince had another change of heart and called off the whole thing. At the time, word in the biz was that when Prince realised the tracks would be too explicit and violent for radio they would not play it, he got cold feet. But the real reason was something far less prosaic.

As Prince later told friends, on the eve of releasing *The Black Album* he'd had a dream in which he experienced a religious vision. 'It was like a born-again thing,' said one. 'He felt this music was way too dark and said if he died, he didn't want this being the last thing representing him.'

So, instead, Prince ordered all the copies of the record to be recalled from distributors and ceremonially destroyed. Inevitably, though, several copies of the finished album survived the cull and went on to have an interesting life as bootlegs. Indeed, the scarcity of the CD turned it overnight into the must-have item for all serous collectors of Prince ephemera.

Eventually, it would even have a semi-official release, allowed out of its long-locked cell finally in 1994. At which point, it was hard not to see it as an ahead-of-the-curve anticipator of the kind of snub-nosed love as anger and violence found in the gangster rap of the early Nineties. Decades on, *The Black Album* has assumed a more benign presence, a naughty but nice album full of decidedly ribald dance tracks like 'Le Grind',

'Superfunkycalifragsexy' and, most naughty of all, the self-parodic and thrillingly danceable instrumental '2 Nigs United 4 West Compton'.

Listening to such tracks now they all seem remarkably tame – exactly what they are: birthday party tracks for grown-ups with a nicely baked sense of humour. Prince didn't see it that way at the time, though: not only pummelling whatever copies of the album he could get his nervous hands on, he flip-flopped and decided to make his real next album a musically dexterous but lyrically straitlaced homage to god and spirituality – and sex, which was the same thing for Prince – called *Lovesexy*.

First though, there was the business of putting the finishing touches to his new heaven-on-earth home, Paisley Park. Named after the single from *Around the World* – key line: 'Love is the colour this place imparts, there aren't any rules in Paisley Park' – this was to be Prince's fortress. On an enormous 70,000 sq ft site, a 20-minute drive down Interstate 5 highway out of the Twin Cities of Minneapolis and St Paul, and situated in amongst the thrusting new premises of software companies in the lush acres of greenery known as Chanhassen, lay Paisley Park.

From outside its fenced grounds, Paisley Park looked not unlike any other vast industrial complex. Inside, however, this was to be Prince's idea of heaven. Within its tall white walls were Prince's luxurious private living quarters, no fewer than three recording studios, fully kitted-out rehearsal rooms, a soundstage within its own concert hall, a 'wardrobe department' overseen by half a dozen employees, including a team of tailors, working round the clock to make bespoke clothes for his band and girlfriends and, of course, the singer himself, plus a full-time hairdressing salon, a makeup room, even his own beautifully lit nightclub replete with VIP balcony, polished chrome stairwell, half-moon tables and crushed-velvet sofas, overlooked by two 20-foot-high screens showing his own videos, and those of others he admired. There were also smaller apartment spaces for special guests, Miles Davis being one of its first visitors to be offered this special brand of hospitality.

The only thing missing from this purple paradise was a fully stocked bar. Prince had been teetotal all of his life. Had famously never done drugs, nor knowingly employed band members who took drugs or drank conspicuously. He didn't even like to stock tea or coffee, though there was always some available for anybody that fancied a cup. And definitely no smoking under any circumstances. Instead, guests would be offered fresh fruit juices or iced glasses of water. Fresh sliced fruit was also freely offered, as were delicate plates of raw vegetables.

Most of what were considered the public rooms were painted purple, and were home to several purple-hued toy clowns and various music boxes and adult toys. And, of course, there was an aircraft-hangar-sized garage that housed several limited-edition supercars, including his day-to-day wheels, a sleek yellow top-of-the-range BMW, and the purple customized 1981 Honda CM400 Hondamatic motorcycle Prince had ridden in *Purple Rain*. Even the toilets at Paisley Park were decorated purple, while the long corridors were festooned with row after row of the dozens of gold, silver and platinum records Prince had received throughout his stellar career, as well as his various Grammy, MTV, BRITS and American Music Awards trophies, and of course his Oscar. The walls of the main reception area were also covered in paintings and murals of the singer.

There was the Galaxy Room, set aside for meditation, softly illuminated, its ceiling alive with hand-painted planets, a mini-indoor universe of the mind. And finally, there was the Knowledge Room, an impressively stocked private library featuring dozens of bibles from around the world and various self-knowledge manuals.

Officially opened on 11 September 1987, at a cost of, by conservative estimates, around $10 million, the most impressive part of the building was, inevitably, the studio where Prince would work exclusively for the rest of his life. Past the pearl and chiffon cage where Prince's droopy-eyed white doves resided, through the gallery over the atrium, with its jukebox and various arcade games, down mink-lined carpets, Studio A was a 48-track analogue (as distinct from digital) set-up. Prince hated computers, allowed his employees to use them only grudgingly, and would never own a mobile phone. For Prince, modern technology counted only for things like keeping his studio amplifiers in a temperature-controlled room, so as not to overheat the studio, as they were kept switched on 24 hours a day. Not just because Prince liked it that way, but because the other two studios, B and C, were booked up by other acts almost all of the time.

As far as Prince was concerned, the most important component in recording was ambience. Hence the six tons of imported hand-cut and hand-polished Italian marble, granite and cherry-wood that lined the studio.

It had taken Prince just ten years to get from recording in the dank basement of a high-school friend's house to a place he considered, he said, 'the kind of place you could invite God in to spend some time'. Surely then the next ten years would find Prince making the most divine music of his career?

9
S-L-A-V-E

If the 1980s had belonged to Prince, the 1990s threatened to get away from him almost from the start. Having ended the decade with two albums of shiny pop simplicity in *Lovesexy* (1988) and the soundtrack to *Batman* (1989), both of which gave him his first No. 1 albums in the UK, it seemed as though Prince had now positioned himself firmly in the mainstream. It wasn't just about pulling *The Black Album* from the schedules because of its 'negativity', even the social comment of *Sign o' the Times* was now only hinted at in passing on otherwise cartoonish tracks like 'Dance On', which mentioned Uzis the way others might mention lollipops. No more songs about the big disease with a little name or gangs of 'disciples' out of their minds on crack and shooting guns. *Lovesexy* came with an all-white cover with a naked Prince depicted a sylph-like shyly concealing his breasts with his hands. The only thing missing was a halo. That and any real hit singles. 'Alphabet Street' was a neat Top 10 hit but nothing else released from the album stuck.

The accompanying tour was a hit, though. No longer bending over backwards trying to fill stadiums, Prince shrewdly gained more column inches for the multiple nights of sell-out arena shows he laid on in London (seven nights at Wembley),

Paris (four nights at the Bercy), four nights in Milan, two nights each in Los Angeles and New York. The stage show was so elaborate though, the stage in two moveable tiers, the props complicated and expensive – including a fountain, a basketball hoop, white trellis fences and a full-size replica of the singer's Ford Thunderbird – that the tour only finally went into the black financially when it reached the final seven-show leg of the tour in Japan.

Prince affected not to care. Why should he? His next project was even more lightweight, the soundtrack to the Tim Burton reboot of the *Batman* movie franchise, starring Michael Keaton, Jack Nicholson and Kim Basinger. The movie was the hot ticket of the summer in the US, where its opening-weekend gross of $46.3 million beat that of the previous record holder, *Ghostbusters*. But purists argued about the plotline, many couldn't understand the Prince soundtrack and even Burton later admitted, 'The whole movie is mainly boring to me. It's OK, but it was more of a cultural phenomenon than a great movie.'

Prince fans lapped up the album, though, thrilled by the video for the lead-off single, 'Batdance', which featured several Bat Girls in skintight costumes and bat ears and Prince himself as a strange good–evil hybrid of the white-faced, green-haired Joker and the heroic, black-faced Batman figure, pointy black cape flapping as he dances around, the whole set bathed in – you guessed it – a fluorescent purple light, and was directed, interestingly, by Albert Magnoli, the first time the two had worked together since the *Purple Rain* movie.

The single went to No. 1 in America and No. 2 in the UK, and the following summer, his commercial fortunes transformed seemingly overnight, Prince embarked on his biggest, most successful tour yet, three months of mainly stadium shows in Britain and Europe, where he had struggled just the year before. Dubbed the Nude tour, it took in sold-out football stadiums across Europe before landing in London for 12 nights at Wembley Arena. Gone were the surreal costumes and over-the-top paraphernalia of the *Lovesexy* tour, replaced by a leaner, meaner greatest-hits show built as a crowd-pleaser of epic proportions.

With his commercial star back in the ascendancy, Prince decided the time was right to try his hand again at being a movie star. *Under the Cherry Moon* may have bombed, but with his name attached to *Batman* it was a good time to parlay a new film deal. To sweeten the deal still further he came up with the ultimate movie producer bait – a proper sequel to *Purple Rain*, no less, along with the return of Morris Day and The Time, plus cameos from Mavis Staples and George Clinton – and, of course, a beautiful new starlet named Ingrid Chavez to play The Kid's love interest, Aura.

Written and directed by Prince, if he'd been hoping that lightning would strike twice, he was sorely mistaken. Instead, the film, titled *Graffiti Bridge*, and shot over the early weeks of 1990, was based on a reed-thin plot essentially just a vehicle to get Prince and his onscreen rivals The Time fighting for musical superiority in a club and moral superiority in Prince's and Morris Day's inevitable squabble over a girl – spoiler alert: the good guy, i.e. Prince, gets the girl and defeats the baddy, Morris, with a song.

Released in November 1990 it was a face-shaming flop that made less than half the meagre money *Under the Cherry Moon* had. Prince would never make a film again. The 17-track CD soundtrack to *Graffiti Bridge*, released four months ahead of the film, also struggled to make an impact, its only hit single, 'Thieves in the Temples', which reached the Top 10 in Britain and America, dragging the album to the upper reaches of the world's charts in its wake.

As had happened before, Prince took this setback the only way he knew how – by making damn sure whatever he did next *was* a success. 1990 was also the year when Sinéad O'Connor took her even-better-than-the-real-thing version of 'Nothing Compares 2 U' to the world in a way not even Prince had imagined possible. O'Connor had reconfigured the lyrics away from a simple breakup song towards a deeper meditation on loss, the singer dedicating the song to her mother, who passed away the same year. It went to No. 1 in America and Britain, and 15 other countries around the world. It was also nominated for three Grammy awards. Prince, who rarely commented on the success other artists had with his songs, was ecstatic. 'I love it, it's great!' he said happily. 'I look for cosmic meaning in everything. I think we just took that song as far as we could, then someone else was supposed to come along and pick it up.'

Fascinated by the Grammy award-winning video that O'Connor filmed to go with it – a remarkable one-shot of O'Connor's face, as she emotes her way through the song, anger, devastation, shock and simple heartbreak all registering like forked lightning across the surface of her moon-shaped face, the sort of deep-contact, bare-bones experience Prince had never achieved on film or video – he invited the famously uncompromising Irish singer to Paisley Park. Prince had always worked so well with female artists, went the thinking, perhaps he had another song he wanted Sinéad to sing, or some other form of collaboration?

But things started to go wrong almost immediately,

O'Connor later claimed. 'I did meet him a couple of times. We didn't get on at all. In fact we had a punch-up.' She explained: 'He summoned me to his house after "Nothing Compares 2 U". I made it without him. I'd never met him. He summoned me to his house – and it's foolish to do this to an Irish woman – he said he didn't like me saying bad words in interviews. So I told him to fuck off.' After which, she said, Prince became 'quite violent. I had to escape out of his house at five in the morning. He packed a bigger punch than mine.'

It became a story O'Connor told more than once in media interviews over the years, though Prince always denied anything like she described took place. Speaking to the Irish music paper *Hot Press*, she said she and Prince had actually had a fist fight. "He's a very frightening person. His windows are covered in tin foil because he doesn't like light." Finally, though, in a TV interview with the chat show host Graham Norton, O'Connor insisted the story was 'much exaggerated by the press' and referred to Prince instead as 'a sweet guy'.

There were much bigger and more important battles ahead for Prince in the Nineties. After restoring his status as a multi-platinum-selling artist with the 1991 album, *Diamonds and Pearls*, including his fifth US No. 1 single, 'Cream', the feeling was still that Prince existed inside his own purple-hued bubble, but at least here was an album without any real agenda outside making great music, its only moment of off-the-hook Prince-style insanity the ferociously funky single 'Gett Off', which promised '23 positions in a one-night stand'.

Yet again Prince seemed to have managed the feat of being darling and mainstream one minute – his breathtaking five-song special on the Arsenio Hall chat show that year remains one of the most extraordinary live performances in American television history – while apparently doing his best to provoke contempt from the 'straights', shocking an audience of millions with his live performance of 'Gett Off' at the MTV Music awards, in which he and his band were surrounded by dozens of near-naked male and female dancers, painted gold and engaged in what for all the world looked like an orgy, albeit in time to the music. When the TV audience could avert its gaze from the dancers long enough to notice, they were confronted by a hip-thrusting Prince in a skintight yellow jumpsuit, with his buttocks on show through some thin nylon gauze.

The *Diamonds and Pearls* tour that took place the following year was another multi-night extravaganza at some of the world's biggest venues, including eight nights at London's cavernous Earl's Court arena. Prince's new band The New Power Generation (NPG) was his most extraordinary creation yet and there was no doubting the power and charisma Prince still exuded on stage, a supernova screeching across the indoor sky. But from here on in, things would start to get seriously weird for both Prince and even his most devoted fans.

The first sign of something being amiss was when Prince's next album, his second and last with the NPG, known colloquially as the *Love Symbol Album*, aka *Love Symbol*, aka simply *Symbol*, didn't actually come with a title but rather a cover adorned with a strange, unpronounceable symbol, copyrighted by Prince under the title Love Symbol No. 2, hence the alternative titles given to the album. Clearly, Prince was sending some sort of message. But what exactly? The music on *Symbol* offered no clue, a promiscuous collection of styles, from the expected funk, R&B and synth-pop, to less expected strands of jazz, reggae, even hip-hop. All were executed with immaculate style but to what purpose remained a mystery as the first two singles – a slinky James Brown-style soul shuffle called 'Sexy MF' and a hard-nosed rap explosion called 'My Name Is Prince' – both hit the UK Top 10 but failed to make the US charts. (Conversely, the third single from the album, a pedestrian pop throwaway titled '7', missed the UK charts but reached No. 7 in the US.)

The only real clues, in retrospect, to what Prince was up to now were in the videos for 'My Name Is Prince' and '7'. In the former his face is concealed beneath an ornately tasselled hat, in the latter a webbed mask. Was Prince, who had enjoyed so many different pseudonyms and aliases over the years playing with the concept of identity again? Yes, he was, only this time he was playing for keeps. The biggest surprise of his never dull career came on 7 June 1993, the day of his thirty-fifth birthday, at a press conference, when he announced that because he had been 'dispossessed in perpetuity' by his record company, he was changing his name to the same unpronounceable symbol that adorned his album. Further, that he would no longer have dealings with any media outlet that continued to use his old name, 'Prince'.

The press were aghast. Half of them had no idea what he was talking about: how record companies own an artist's work in perpetuity, receiving by far the biggest share of the profits of that artist's work, and have ultimate control over what the artist releases and even how often. The half of the press that did know what Prince was alluding to couldn't believe that an artist who had just signed a new contract with Warner's reportedly worth in the region of $100 million could consider himself hard done by, whatever the royalty–control split. The most bewildering problem for them, though, in the short term, was how to write about this new development without addressing Prince as, well, Prince.

But Prince even had an answer for that. His company issued software with new fonts on it so that newspapers and magazines could go on reporting about Prince but under his new – unpronounceable, unspellable – name. For those who couldn't get the font, they were instructed that the following abbreviation would be acceptable: O(+>). For those who couldn't manage that, Prince let it be known that he was happy simply to be known as 'The Artist Formerly Known as Prince'. The ban was dismissed as another publicity stunt, but the laughter stopped abruptly when it emerged that he was also extending this prohibition on the use of his name to group members and friends. They would have to do with simply referring to him as The Artist.

Was Prince – sorry, O(+>) – serious? Very serious indeed, apparently, explaining at the press conference that he was so disturbed by the situation he found himself in that it had provoked a full-on identity crisis. 'I would wake up at nights thinking: "Who am I?"' he said mournfully.

It soon became evident, however, that the chief issue Prince had with Warner's was their attempt to keep him from releasing too much new product all at once. Mo Ostin, for so long Prince's champion at the company, had decided not to renew his contract with Warner's and would officially leave in 1994. Whatever battles Prince envisaged having with his record label, Mo would no longer be the guy to help him out. While Russ Thyret, who had originally been so instrumental in signing Prince, and would effectively take over leading Warner's as CEO in 1995, took the same position as practically every other single person in the music business, and

argued that under the terms of the $100 million contract
Prince had signed just months before declaring he wanted out
of the deal, Prince should have been the wealthiest – and most
grateful – artist in recording history. That he was not was perhaps simply one demand too many for the company-minded
new CEO.

Prince though was not a company man. He was an artist.
No longer satiated by giving what extra material he had to
other artists – both established and newly made up by him
– and increasingly frustrated at the huge archive of material
he had catalogued at Paisley Park that he feared no one would
hear, Prince had gone to Warner's and discussed a plan to release up to three, maybe four, new albums a year, along with a
blur of one-off singles and multi-track EPs.

This was at a time, it should be remembered, when record
labels, grown fat on the sale of overpriced CDs, had devised
a well-worn path for its major artists to follow. Ideally, an
artist of the stature of Prince would release at most one new
album every two years, from which the label would extract
up to seven singles, possibly even more, while the artist dil-
igently toured the world for the commercial lifespan of the
album. That was the formula and one the major labels of the
world, including Warner's, were determined to stick to. Prince
had already been indulged they felt, by allowing him to release
one new album every year; to try and push that further by
releasing two or three or god almighty four albums a year was
simply insane, commercial suicide. Indeed, they would have
rather Prince take a leaf out of Bruce Springsteen's book, his
own 1992 album, *Human Touch*, having been his first for five
years. Or Michael Jackson's, whose 1991 album, *Dangerous*,
was his first for four years, and only his second since *Thriller* a

decade before. Or even Madonna's, whose 1992 album, *Erotica*, was her first for three years.

But Prince wasn't like the others, didn't they know that yet? Warner's exec Ted Cohen tried to put the problem into terms people could understand in an interview some years later with *Billboard*, when he explained: 'Warner treated him like a God but they weren't set up to do what you can do today with digital. He was so prolific [that he] wanted to record something on Monday and release it by Friday. He would record in April and it would be released in September for an October or November tour. He hated that. It wasn't about royalties.'

Cohen went on: 'He wanted to release stuff as he created it. He didn't want to be caught up with the construct of five songs on an EP or 10 songs on an LP. He believed – there was a strong concern – that he would create something new but by the time it came to market any artist on the street that heard him play in a club would appropriate what he created and by the time he released it, it would sound like he was them.'

This latter point may have been somewhat paranoid, but other artists, including many whom Prince had helped early in their careers, had been copying him for years. Or at the very least trying to keep up. The larger point though was one that Prince was absolutely determined to hold to. He was an artist, not a popsicle machine, he should be allowed to let the public hear his latest creations while they were still fresh to him. But Warner's like all major record companies in the Nineties were not there to be innovative, they were there to make money. What Prince was proposing, they told him, would kill his sales, muddy his public profile and simply confuse whatever message he was trying to get out there to his fans.

On this point they would be proved right as over the next

few years Prince's record sales dried up to the point where he could no longer guarantee high chart placings in Britain, America or anywhere else in the world. He would have occasional big-sellers, one-off triumphs that kept him in the public eye and maintained his status as one of the world's greatest live performers. But just as Warner's had feared, the name-change had proved off-putting, confusing. How on earth did you go into a record store and ask for the new album by . . . what? Squiggle?

Prince as ever seemed to take a perverse delight in confusing the public, even when it was obviously in fun. Interviewed on the cable TV show *The Sunday Show*, in March 1995, Prince appeared on the show in a hat, his face completely hidden behind an ornately bejewelled scarf. He had agreed to be interviewed, the presenter Veronica Webb explained, on two conditions: that he would not speak or show his face. Instead Mayte Garcia, seated next to him, would be his 'interpreter'. It was a bizarre spectacle that was highly amusing but, frustratingly, maddeningly short on explanations as to why he no longer wished to be called Prince – or even show his face on what was his first TV interview for ten years.

Webb began by asking: 'Now what's the reason to give an interview and not speak?'

Prince held up a newspaper, with the headline, which she read out:

'Prince is dead – Long live rock's tiny sex symbol.'

He nodded. She went on: 'So Prince has nothing to say, and the Artist Formerly Known as Prince is for ever in silence, which I suppose is golden. But don't you think you're blowing your chance for people to understand what your case is, why you won't speak?'

Prince whispered something to Mayte. She passed it on: 'He never blows chances.'

Veronica Webb: 'Well, there you go. That's incredible confidence, but how do you expect people to be sympathetic to what's going on with you if they can't understand your situation?'

More whispering. Mayte: 'Next question.'

And so it went. Eventually, in less spangled contexts, Prince would be more serious. 'Once Warner's refused to sell me my masters, I was faced with a problem,' he told *USA Today*. 'But "pro" is the prefix of problem, so I decided to do something about it.'

In an in-depth interview with *Details*, when asked what was wrong with being on Warner's, he laid it all on the line at last. 'I like to go with my intuition. Something hits me and I need to get the track down before I can move on. It's like there's another person inside me, talking to me, and I'm learning to listen to that voice.'

He added: 'It's a way of cutting the chaos off, cutting off the outside voices. I heard "Prince is crazy" so much that it had an effect on me. So one day I said, "Let me just check out." Here [at Paisley Park] there is solitude, silence – I like to stay in this controlled environment. People say I'm out of touch, but I'll do 25 or 30 more albums – I'm gonna catch up with Sinatra – so you tell me who's out of touch. One thing I ain't gonna run out of is music.'

He still had a hard time convincing anyone, though, that he was anybody's 'slave'. If Prince had been a figure of fun to a certain degree at the height of his fame, just as Elvis, The Beatles and David Bowie had before him, by the mid-Nineties it was open season on Prince. Who did he think he was? What was it he was supposed to be achieving? What was his name again?

There were exceptions, of course. New Prince music that was simply too good, too undeniable, for anyone to care who it was supposed to be by. When he released a new single, in 1994, titled 'The Most Beautiful Girl in the World', it became Prince's first and only No. 1 single in the UK, as well as becoming a huge hit around the world. A lush, almost too-delicate-to-touch ballad written for the new love of Prince's life, Mayte (pronounced my-tie) Garcia, 20 years old and the star dancer in Prince's latest live show. It showed once again just how incredibly talented Prince was – and, even more importantly to him, how he could still have massive hit records even without a name. The ads for the single still maintained the façade that 'Prince' was no more, The Artist pictured lounging in a chair with a hat pulled down over his face, and Garcia standing sylph-like next to his chair.

When he turned up at the 1995 BRIT awards to receive the award for Best International Male Artist he did so with the word S-L-A-V-E stencilled on the right cheek of his face. There to promote his latest album, *The Gold Experience*, though we didn't know it then it'd be his last that would reach the Top 10 in Britain or America for nearly a decade, Prince stood at the podium in yellow suit and black shades, and viewed the audience thoughtfully. When he spoke, he did so only in coded messages. 'Prince . . . the best?' He cocked his head quizzically. '*The Gold Experience* . . . In concert, perfectly free . . . On record – slave.' He smiled then became serious again. 'Get wild. Come. Peace. Thank you.' Then a quick wave and he was gone, to screams.

When Blur went up to receive one of the four awards they

received that night, their drummer, Dave Rowntree, had taken a felt-tip pin and drawn the word D-A-V-E on his face. Prince looked on from his table stony-faced. But many industry insiders present made it clear they found the joke hilarious. Prince, though, held firm. Two years later when he returned to the BRITS to perform live, he no longer had 'slave' on his face but he was still insisting he be known only as The Artist. But by then people had given up even trying to understand what the hell was going on there.

For Prince, though, it wasn't the viewing audience back home he was aiming his message at, but the bigwigs in the room. As he explained to the *Icon* magazine writer Touré, 'Imagine yourself sitting in a room with the biggest of the big in the recording industry, and you have "Slave" written on your face. That changes the entire conversation. They said, "It makes it real hard to talk to you with that on your face." I said, "Why?" And it got real quiet. Adding that language into the conversation worked perfectly. It changed the dynamic.'

The trouble was the folks back home who were watching on TV and did have an opinion, and not always a very flattering one. In fact, a great many black Americans found nothing funny at all about the sight of one of their leading black entertainers walking around with the word 'slave' on his face. Prince's lawyer at the time, and the man who would eventually help Prince get out of his Warner's contract, L. Londell McMillan, talked in 1998 about how he himself was deeply offended by the word 'slave' being on anybody's face, let alone someone with such a huge profile as Prince. 'The reference is traumatic to African-Americans,' he explained in an interview with *Q* magazine in 1998. 'In one of my first conversations with him I said, "Take the 'Slave' off your face." He said, "Get me free of this contract and I will." It became clear that he was a desperate man.'

As one Warner's executive from that time put it, 'We were adhering to the terms of the contract, we were paying him millions, how could we be slave masters?', a view that the respected black music journalist Nelson George shared: 'He was less a slave and had more artistic freedom than any black artist I know of!'

The hardest battle Prince fought in the mid-Nineties though concerned his personal life. Mayte Garcia first came to Prince's attention in 1990, at the age of 17, when her ambitious mother, Nelle, sent him a videotape of her daughter dancing. The daughter of a US Air Force major, of Puerto Rican descent, Mayte had been a belly-dancer since the age of three and a professional dancer since she was eight – when she appeared on the US TV show *That's Incredible!* as the world's youngest professional belly dancer. Growing up in America and Germany, where her father was stationed, she had just graduated from the General H. H. Arnold High School in Wiesbaden when Prince first met her on tour in Germany – hiring her a year later to dance on the *Diamonds and Pearls* tour.

Prince began his affair with her around this time, though he did his best to keep it hidden from the press. Close friends said he was besotted by Mayte, but were still surprised when he based much of the lyrical focus of the *Love Symbol* album on her, in the unexpected guise of an Egyptian princess, even getting her to add her vocals to certain tracks – in English and Spanish – and co-starring in the accompanying movie clips and music direct-to-video *3 Chains o' Gold*.

When Prince's love song to Mayte, 'The Most Beautiful Girl in the World', went to No. 1 around the world, there was intense tabloid speculation that the two were actually about to get married. But when Prince responded to a question from a reporter in 1994 about whether he would settle down and have a family of his own one day by saying, 'I decided that things like family don't have a big part to play in my future. I'm dedicated to music, to the point that I see all of life through it', it seemed that was that.

Then, suddenly, on Valentine's Day in 1996, Prince and Mayte were married. Fans were even more agog when he then spoke openly about his wedding night to *Hello!* magazine. 'Mayte was still wearing her long white dress when I brought her into the bedroom and played her my new song "Let's Have A Baby",' he told Solange Plamindon. 'She couldn't stop crying – it was an unforgettable moment.' Prince, in his usual over-the-top romantic style, had a crib next to the marriage bed. Then within weeks it was announced that Mayte was, in fact, pregnant.

A baby boy, named Boy Gregory, was born on 16 October that year. The couple were ecstatic. Then completely devastated when Boy Gregory died just seven days later, the victim of the rare cranial disorder Pfeiffer syndrome – a condition characterized by the premature fusion of certain bones of the skull which affects the shape of the head and face, often a high prominent forehead and eyes that bulge. Beside himself with grief and almost a sense of disbelief, Prince seemed to be in extreme denial when just a few days after Gregory's death, as a guest on Oprah Winfrey's show, he told her the baby was doing fine. He then told a press conference how much he was 'enjoying fatherhood'. Months later, when quizzed on this disturbing behaviour he tried to brush it off by explaining, somewhat disingenuously, that it was based on an old family superstition that he once wove into a song's lyrics. To wit: 'If you ever lose someone dear to you, never say the words "They're gone" and they'll come back.' But it was clear he was near to losing his mind with grief.

Neither Prince nor Mayte ever got over their loss. They thought they still had a chance for happiness when Mayte became pregnant for a second time some months later. But when she lost that baby to an unfortunate miscarriage, the couple never recovered – and in 1999 their marriage was annulled on their third wedding anniversary. Garcia next embarked on a two-year relationship with Mötley Crüe's drummer Tommy Lee, though she maintained in interviews that she would always love her ex-husband. She later carved a career out for herself as a choreographer and actress, famously working on the video for Britney Spears's 2001 song 'I'm a Slave 4 U', with Garcia choreographing the sexy belly-dancing routines performed by Spears and her backing dancers.

Prince, for his part, was now in his early forties and being forced to reappraise his life. When both his parents died in 2001, friends worried that he would fall back into depression. Prince had stayed close to both his parents, inviting his father to contribute musical ideas to various albums in recent years, all of which he was credited and paid extremely well for, and making sure his mother was taken care of, being by her bed-side when she died. Prince, whose own attempt at having a family had ended so tragically with the death of his own only child, felt the loss of his parents deeply. He still had his sibling and step-siblings, but to them he had become the father figure. Who would he now look to for guidance in the quiet hours?

Instead of brooding for too long though, he bounced back, determined to make the twenty-first century his own. A settlement was finally reached with Warner's in April 1996, with Prince's contract to end a couple of albums earlier than originally agreed back when the deal was thought to be worth more than $100 million, final terms binding and undisclosed. There would be just one more album under the old 'slave' contract: *Chaos and Disorder*, a ragbag of outtakes and oddities that would barely sell 100,000 copies. 'The day I received Warner's countersignature,' McMillan told the British writer Phil Sutcliffe, who had so brilliantly covered much of those chaotic years for The Artist, 'I asked him if he was ready to go to the bathroom and wipe it off and he said, "I'm ready", and he did it.'

Prince certainly felt free the moment the record deal ended. 'It's like eighteen orgasms at once,' he said. By 1999, his Warner–Chappell publishing contract had also expired. 'That's the last contract in existence with my name on it,' he stated.

But amidst the ballyhoo and celebrations, there was still business to take care of. Though he was loath to discuss it or even admit to the rumours in public, word round the campfire was that Prince was actually in financial trouble. Yes, he was free of Warner's. But by the end of the Nineties his Warner-distributed Paisley Park label had also expired, along with specialist Prince-owned merchandising shops in London, Miami and Minneapolis. His live shows could still make him upwards of $300,000 a night, but his records didn't sell like they had in his heyday. 'For me, the album is already a success when I have a copy,' he claimed defiantly in a *Rolling Stone* interview. '*Lovesexy* is supposed to be a failure, but I go on the Internet and someone says, "*Lovesexy* saved my life."'

Nevertheless, none of the six albums he'd released between 1995 and 2001 had been a major hit, the most recent, *The*

Rainbow Children, only scraping to No. 109 in the US, while not registering at all anywhere else in the world, including Britain.

There had been some mighty high moments along the way – the cheeky title track of the 1994 album, *Come*; the immortal 'The Most Beautiful Girl in the World from *The Gold Experience*; the delightful guitar-pop of 'Dinner With Dolores' from the otherwise pedestrian *Chaos and Disorder* – but by 1996 it was rumoured that Madonna had secretly offered him a rescue merger with her Maverick Records label, but he was indignant at the very suggestion.

'That's not true,' he insisted. 'We haven't talked in years.' Nevertheless, by the end of the Nineties the rumours were that Prince was actually hovering on the edge of bankruptcy. Again, he furiously refuted such claims, pointing to the relative success of his outlandish, 53-track five-CD box set *Crystal Ball/The Truth*; although it only reached No. 62 in the US and No. 91 in Britain (and absolutely nowhere at all anywhere else in the world). 'People say the marketing of *Crystal Ball* through the Internet went wrong, but we sold 250,000 plus at $50 each.'

But then Prince's relationship with the so-called real world had always been tenuous at best. Now as a middle-aged man who'd been told he was a superstar since he was 19, he would often come unstuck even in his dealings with other superstars. During his early years at war with Warner's, he had reached out to George Michael, who was going through a similar legal battle for 'freedom' with his label, Sony. But the former Wham! singer seemed baffled, even affronted by the approach. 'He lacks a certain social grace,' confessed Prince's British PR at the time, the estimable Chris Poole. Another time, by

Prince's own account, he approached REM's frontman and fellow Warner's superstar Michael Stipe at a party in London and without bothering to introduce himself or even say hello first, asked him for his thoughts. 'I said, "Do you own your masters?" He looked scared. He started stuttering. He said, "I don't know." I said, "You need to and you should help me get mine." He just said, "Have a nice day." That was it . . .'

Was Prince, perhaps, feeling that perverse sense of hurrying to stand still familiar to a great many men as they turn from their still-youthful thirties to their no-denying-it-now 'mature' forties? Or, to put it more plainly, were his best days behind him now?

But, of course, Prince regarded such a suggestion as ridiculous, if not insulting. 'I love growing older,' he said in a contemporary interview with *The Times*. 'You can figure things out quicker because you've seen how things happen in the past and so you watch the results a certain action will have. Also, the older I get the closer I am to where I'm going, which is a better place.' Getting into his stride, he went on: 'We all have a purpose within us. We are put here for a reason. My talent is God-given, but the music is made by me. I make the choices that make the music.'

The first album he released following his victory over Warner's, on his own NPG Records label, distributed through EMI, was called, suitably, *Emancipation*. And it was his best work in years, even Prince agreed with that. It was also his most successful, even if that term was now more relative, reaching No. 11 in the US and No. 18 in the UK. A triple album, no less, and his third album to be released that year, alongside his last for Warner's, the largely throwaway *Chaos and Disorder*, and the soundtrack for the Spike Lee movie *Girl 6*, *Emancipation* tried hard to sound like an artistic comeback, while equally insisting he'd never been away. Tellingly, of its 36 tracks, only one, a virtual note-for-note cover of the 1972 hit for The Sylistics 'Betcha By Golly Wow', came close to being a hit, creeping into the UK Top 30, but not even registering in America.

Prince didn't care. He was now free and that meant more to him than all the hit records in the world. As he told *Musician* in 1997, 'I had to take some [of the *Emancipation*] songs, like "A Thousand Hugs and Kisses" and "She Gave Her Angels" off the Warner albums because they were all about the same subject. But now I can write a song that says, "If u ask God 2 love u longer, every breath u take will make u stronger, keepin' u happy and proud 2 call His name: Jesus" [from 'The Holy River' on *Emancipation*], and not have to worry about what *Billboard* magazine will say. Plus I'm not splitting the earnings up with anyone else except the people who deserve to have them. The people here in my studio will reap the benefits of how *Emancipation* does, not people in some office somewhere who didn't contribute anything to the music.'

Prince, it seemed, had his career exactly where he wanted it, at last. But to get there he'd had to sacrifice so much career momentum there were now serious questions about where this would all ultimately lead, as we exchanged one millennium for another. Prince said he was ready for the future. But were we?

10

Freedom!

The new century brought the dawning of a new age for Prince. In his forties, his long, damaging battle with Warner's over, now looking at a life beyond his tragic first marriage and the death of his parents, Prince was in crisis as he struggled with depression and the feeling that the best part of his life was over. In search of a renewed sense of purpose that he knew in his heart it would take more than just another hit album or tour to find, he turned to religion. Not the kind of sex-is-God-is-freedom rollercoaster he'd been on these past 20 years, but something more formal. Something that came with a tangible set of principles, of hard-and-fast rules that anybody could follow. If there was no one left on Earth who could tell him what to do, he would have to find that voice – that sense of the strong father and giving mother – of an all-powerful God that wasn't of his own creation, but already existed.

Prince's mother, Mattie, who had died just six months after his father, John, passed away, in 2001, gave as her final wish that her son should become a Jehovah's Witness as she had been for most of her life – and that he would be married. Prince was still mulling that over when God seemed to give him a sign, he said, in the form of the one-time Sly & The Family Stone bassist Larry Graham. Prince had been friends with

Larry for years, claiming he'd been more influenced by Graham's post-Sly band, Graham Central Station, than he had the Family Stone. Prince had even signed Larry to his fledgling NPG label, in the years immediately following getting out of his Warner's contract, producing a highly regarded solo album, *GCS2000*.

Now though, seeing how afraid and unsure his friend was, Graham came to Prince and began speaking of his own long-time experience as a Jehovah's Witness, crediting the religion with helping him overcome years of drug abuse from his own time as a rock star in the Seventies. When Larry, then 55, spoke to Prince about being born again as a Jehovah's Witness, the singer became convinced that that's what he should do too.

'Larry goes door to door to tell people the truth about God,' explained Prince. 'That's why I told myself I need to know a man like him. He's a friend who calls me his baby brother.' According to Graham, 'Prince is a spiritual man. Sometimes we study for hours – six, seven, eight hours a day. We sit down and get into the scriptures.'

The two men would work and pray together at the Chanhassen Congregation, in Kingdom Hall, a few miles from Paisley Park. Speaking to the the *Mirror*, in 2010, Ronald Scofield, one of the Congregation elders there, said, 'We have watched Prince since he started studying the Bible and noticed a dramatic change. We go on Bible studies together and work in field service, the door-to-door ministry that Jehovah's Witnesses are known for. When people being called on get past the initial shock of actually meeting Prince, he is very persuasive. He uses the scriptures very well.'

The effect on Prince of his conversion to Jehovah was astonishing. Suddenly he found new energy, but not in the all-or-nothing way of the past. He still needed to feel he was in control of his environment, whether working with his band or at home with friends, but he no longer ruled with an iron fist. He had finally found a balance between work and play. Suddenly other people and their own lives mattered again, both onstage – gone were the days of the over-elaborate stage shows, replaced by tightly rehearsed but much looser band performances: 'There's no more envelope to push,' he announced. 'I pushed it off the table. It's on the floor. Let's move forward' – and off it. Suddenly there was a new love in Prince's life. Not a dancer or singer or would-be celebrity in her own right, but a beautiful, down-to-earth girl named Manuela Testolini.

'Mani', as she became known, was 24 years old, willowy and softly spoken when she met Prince while working for his charitable foundation. Within weeks of their first date, Prince had asked her to marry him. The native Canadian largely avoided the spotlight during her marriage to the star, focusing on her charitable endeavours as well as her production company, Gamillah, Inc., which she used to help promote non-profit organizations. Manuela also became a Jehovah's Witness, baptised in a pool, and would attend Bible studies with her new husband at their local Kingdom Hall meeting place. She also accompanied her husband on his weekly outings, knocking on the doors of the astonished residents of Minneapolis. 'To see him in a Christian lifestyle is very pleasant,' said Schofield, who also joined the couple occasionally on these excursions. 'He's doing very well and spiritually he seems to be making a great deal of progress, too.'

Another great change during this period found Prince forging a new life with Mani beyond the walls of his Paisley Park fortress. Maybe the place just held too many sad memories of

Mayte and baby Gregory, who knows? But Prince now preferred to spend his time with his second wife in LA, or chilling out at their luxurious $5 million grey stone mansion in upmarket Toronto – just a five-minute drive from where Mani's parents lived in their small apartment. Setting aside any reservations they may have had over their daughter's much older husband and his exceedingly colourful past, Mani's family appeared to welcome Prince into their fold. When her sister Daniela married in the village of Calabogie, near Ottawa, Prince and Mani arrived in a limousine, before proceeding to cheerfully mingle with family and friends at the reception.

Musically, Prince's style also changed dramatically. His first new album for two years, *The Rainbow Children*, released in November 2001, was a first on many levels. His first album released on his NPG label not supported by a major-label distributor, it was a deliberately low-key affair, its 68 minutes of music rarely reaching the intensity normally associated with a Prince album. His first album since becoming a Jehovah's Witness, lyrically the concerns were built on the same old sex-=spirituality axis, but with the added gloss of a purely Jehovian perspective – the rainbow holding special significance for Jehovah's Witnesses, based on the Bible story of God promising Noah he would never destroy the world with floods again. To wit: 'I promise that never again will all people and animals be destroyed by a flood. I am putting my rainbow in the clouds. And when the rainbow appears, I will see it and remember this promise of mine.'

The music is rich but subdued, full of jazz stylings and restrained rhythms, smooth in all but its meanings, not hidden, but right out there for all the world to see. 'Like a thief in the night,' Prince intones on 'Muse 2 the Pharaoh', 'My Lord come and strike / Leave nothing but ashes to the left, dust to the right . . .'

The musical equivalent of going round town knocking on doors, seeing who might be interested but leaving quietly if not, *The Rainbow Children* was wonderfully understated, beautifully played, but lyrically uncompromising. Made, it would seem, like those knocks on the door, knowing there would be few uptakes, but for those that did, a lot of pretty good stuff to absorb. If that was your trip . . .

In chart terms, people largely ignored *The Rainbow Children*, the album barely registering. The follow-up, though, *One Nite Alone*, fared even less well commercially. This time Prince was alone at the piano, with only a drummer, John Blackwell, contributing to two of the tracks, and the mood is even more sombre and meditative than on *Rainbow's Children*. It's actually a beautifully realized piece of work, but a million miles from anything his mainstream pop audience of the Eighties and early Nineties would recognise. Prince, it seemed, was no longer turned on by the thought of beating Michael Jackson and Madonna at their own games, he had moved into the realm of Miles Davis and John Coltrane. This was Prince taking his music to a new astral plane, to a place where his name really didn't matter as much as his message.

Prince's next two albums, both released in 2003, both again released only via his NPG label website, were even more out there and extraordinary. With the first, the all-instrumental *Xpectation*, we were now into full-on experimental jazz. Available initially as an MP3-only file, it came with no outer sleeve, no credits, no explanations, nothing bar the music, dig if you will. It was the same scenario with *N.E.W.S.*, which followed six months later. If you liked jazz these were the albums for you. But most Prince fans did not.

Things finally seemed to click back into gear for Prince the rock star when to the surprise of everyone he agreed to a special performance opening the Grammy Awards ceremony in February 2004. It began with a full band and orchestra playing the soaring refrain to 'Purple Rain', as Prince stood alone with his guitar, in a purple suit, at the microphone. Then just as he'd finished a chorus, out from the wings came Beyoncé, strutting into view in a short, figure-hugging, sparkly pink dress, with tassels edging the skirt. The show then segued into 'Baby, I'm a Star', Prince discarding the guitar to dance and sing along with Beyoncé. Then just when you thought things couldn't get any camper, band and orchestra transitioned into 'Crazy in Love', four backing singers and dancers heaving into view around Beyoncé.

The segment ended with a double-speed 'Let's Go Crazy', which Prince brought to a rousing, old-school showbiz finale, wailing on his guitar like Hendrix taking a bath as Beyoncé did the funky town fandango next to him, hair twirling and skirt blowing up around her hips. 'Don't hate us cos we fabulous!' Prince exclaimed hurling his guitar in the air as he skipped past her, Beyoncé throwing back her fabulous head and laughing.

'I was really curious as to how much she knew musically,' Prince revealed in a later interview. 'I was really pleased to find out that she knew a lot about scales – mixolydian scales and Egyptian styles.' Was he kidding? Apparently not, going on to explain how he'd shown her some piano chords too, because knowing the instrument had been such a great help to singers like Aretha Franklin and Ray Charles. (Are you *sure* he wasn't kidding?)

It was the same but different story a few months later when Prince was inducted into the Rock and Roll Hall of Fame. When the televised show's producer, Joel Gallen, suggested Prince come and play guitar in a stellar one-off tribute performance to the late Beatles guitarist George Harrison – where he would be joined on stage by Tom Petty, Jeff Lynne, Steve Winwood and Harrison's son, Dhani – Prince surprised the producer by saying yes. The song chosen for the performance was one of Harrison's most famous Beatles tunes, 'While My Guitar Gently Weeps'.

Gallen recalled how during rehearsals Jeff Lynne's guitarist, Marc Mann, stepped forward for the middle guitar break of the song and re-created Eric Clapton's solo note for note. 'And we get to the big end solo,' Gallen said, 'and Prince again steps forward to go into the solo, and this guy starts playing that solo too!'

Prince, who might once have been expected to go into a giant huff and storm off the stage, was entirely cool about the situation though when Gallen sought him out afterwards to reassure him he would be allowed to take the finale solo on the night of the actual show, telling Gallen to let Mann take the first solo, then he would take over for the second, climactic solo at the end of the song. There were no further rehearsals, Prince just assured everyone he would be fine on the night. 'The rest is history,' said Gallen. 'It became one of the most satisfying musical moments in my history of watching and producing live music.'

Indeed it did, with Prince, in a bright red Stetson cowboy hat, not only outgunning Mann with his virtuosity but stealing the entire show away from the other main figures on the stage. According to Tom Petty, speaking afterwards and still grinning from ear to ear, 'You see me nodding at him, to say, "Go on, go on." I remember I leaned out at him at one point and gave him a "This is going great!" kind of look. He just burned it up. You could feel the electricity of something really big's going down here.'

The only thing no one could explain was what happened to Prince's guitar after he threw it up on the air at the end of his solo. As you can still see from the YouTube video of the show, it gets thrown in the air – but never comes back down. 'Everybody wonders where that guitar went,' said Petty's drummer, Steve Ferrone. 'I was astonished that it didn't come back down again, and I gotta tell you, I was on the stage, and I wonder where it went, too.'

Still nothing could quite match the moment when Prince accepted his induction into the Hall of Fame personally from Alicia Keys, flanked by Andre 2000 and Big Boi from Outkast, a group clearly steeped in Prince musical lore. Keys's speech welcoming Prince to the podium was the most heartfelt and memorable of the night.

'There are many kings,' she began, slowly, smilingly, eyes straight into camera. 'King Henry the Eighth, King Solomon, King Tut, King James, King Kong. The Three Kings.' She paused, gave it a beat. 'But there is only *one* Prince.' Cue a round of applause, as the camera came in tight on her face. 'Only one man who has defied restriction. Who has defied the obvious and all the rules to the game. A mysterious figure who when a river of words will not suffice can only be identified by a symbol. Whose music is like an internal rollercoaster that takes each individual on their own separate legendary ride. And still takes listen after listen to discover and uncover even half of the story behind the intriguing and unapologetically addictive beat of music. Yes, ladies and gentlemen, there is only *one* Prince. There's only one man who is so loud he makes you soft, so strong he makes you weak, so honest you feel kind of bashful. So bold he defies you to be subtle, and so superbad he makes you feel so super good. He's the only man that I've ever seen that lights the stage on fire, leaving you to burn within it in a frenzy of movement, lights, electric guitars, slides, pianos, dances, voices, *splits* – and songs. Oh my god, songs so powerful that you are forever changed. Songs that make you laugh and cry, think and dance. Songs that made *me* look at songwriting as stories that are untold passions dying to be heard.

'Because of him I've never wanted to be like anyone else but myself. And because of his music my music has wings to be different. He is the inspiration that generations will return to until the end of time. So, yes, ladies and gentlemen, throughout history there have been many, many kings, both real and mythological. They have borne sons but *none* of them can touch the rays from this man who stands alone. A man who I am tremendously proud and honoured to help induct into the Rock and Roll Hall of Fame tonight, because *now* it is for ever changed. Ladies and gentlemen, I want you to get on your feet and I want you to pay homage to the one and only Prince!'

The place erupted into cheers and hoots and wave after wave of applause as Prince, dressed in a pale lemon suit, black shirt and breast hanky, strode to the stage, no minders, no game face, just . . . himself. By the time he'd reached the podium, the place was giving him such a prolonged standing ovation he asked them to 'Please . . . be seated.'

They did so, reluctantly, and a smiling, clearly easy-within-his-own-skin Prince said simply: 'All praise and thanks to the most high Jehovah.' Then he turned to Alicia and friends: 'I want to thank you, Alicia, Andrew, Big Boi – much respect to you all. Thank you Rock and Roll Hall of Fame, this is definitely an honour. I don't wanna take up too much time but I would just like to say this. When I first started out in this music industry, I was most concerned with freedom. Freedom to produce, freedom to play all the instruments on my records. Freedom to say anything I wanted to. And after much negotiation Warner Brothers Records granted me that freedom and I thank them for that.' Big round of applause. 'Without any real spiritual mentors other than artists whose records I admired, Larry Graham being one of them,' he said nodding towards his friend and fellow Jehovah's Witness in the audience, 'I embarked on a journey more fascinating than I could ever have imagined. But a word to the wise, without real spiritual mentoring, too much freedom can lead to the soul's decay. And a word to the young artists, a real friend and mentor is not on your payroll . . .' Huge applause. 'A real friend and mentor cares for your soul as much as they do their own. This world and its wicked system will become harder and harder to deal with without a real friend and a mentor. And I wish all of you the best on this fascinating journey. It ain't over. Peace.'

There was another standing ovation as Prince made his way back to his table. It was a genuinely moving moment. No more masks, no more teasing, just the real deal, Prince seemed to be saying, could you handle that, baby?

On tour again, Prince now used the clip of Alicia's Hall of Fame speech to play to the audience before he came onstage. He also expunged from his set those songs that had come to, not embarrass him, he felt, but diminish him: 'Head', 'Darling Nikki', 'Gett Off' . . . all gone. Indeed, his 2004 album, a return to more Princely musical styles titled *Musicology*, was something of a homage to monogamy. 'Shame on you, baby,' he sings at one point, 'Can't you see this ring?' In a revealing interview with the American writer Anthony DeCurtis, Prince declared, 'This culture is in big trouble. All you see on television are debased images.' Before going on to express his distaste at the infamous 'wardrobe malfunction' episode of Janet Jackson's Superbowl performance that year, when one of her breasts, suspiciously adorned for the occasion with a nipple-shield, 'accidentally' became exposed.

2004 was a big year for Prince. He hated the word 'comeback', but when *Musicology*, under a new distribution deal between NPG and Columbia, reached the Top 5 of the album charts in America, Britain, Germany and several other countries, getting a Grammy nomination along the way, that's what it felt like to his fans. Prince, though he would never have put it that way himself, seemed to acknowledge as much when at the end of the title track to *Musicology* he added snippets of 'Kiss', 'Little Red Corvette', 'Sign o' the Times', '17 Days' and 'If I Was Your Girlfriend'. Prince was quoted as saying he hoped the album would provide a musical education for his audience. Cool and suave – and knowing and funny – as ever.

'When I became a symbol, all the writers were cracking funnies, but I was the one laughing,' Prince told *Newsweek*. 'I knew I'd be here today, feeling each new album is my first.' Or as he told DeCurtis, 'My fans bring their sons and daughters to my shows now. That's how I grew up. I hope to be an inspiration to those people.' Before concluding: 'I feel at peace. I knew it would take time, and I had to deal with a lot of ridicule. But this feels like peace right now. Spiritually I feel very different from the way I used to, but physically? Not at all.'

That may have been so but clearly Prince was displaying

all the telltale signs of a former tearaway now settling into middle age. There were two more albums released in 2004, but neither of them had major-label distribution and so neither of them charted anywhere. It was a pattern he repeated over the next ten years, releasing albums through NPG either with major-label distribution deals – and therefore becoming chart hits – or not, and therefore not making even a blip on the world's charts, no matter what their actual musical content. Yet when he came to play live, now, like the rest of the major music artists left in the world, he was wise enough to stick to the hits.

This paid off for him – and us – big time when he agreed to headline the Super Bowl halftime show at the 70,000-capacity Sun Life Stadium, in Miami, in February 2007. With a worldwide television audience of over 100 million, performing at the halftime show has become the dream ticket for any rock star worth the title. The Rolling Stones have done it, Beyoncé, U2, The Who, Madonna and of course Michael Jackson. Prince's mission, he decided, was to top them all. Meeting with the show's producers, Prince had clearly done his homework, poring over recordings of the best of the past performances, deciding what he liked and didn't like, and how he could best them.

As Charles Coplin, vice-president of programming for the NFL, explained, 'We look for acts that resonate with the largest possible demographic, from eight to 80 years old. We want artists where their catalogue is familiar but at the same time they're culturally relevant. They're very understanding of the nuances of doing the Superbowl as opposed to doing their own concert. They're innovative and spectacular. It's the most-watched show in the world. That makes it challenging.'

Prince was certainly the Super Bowl's most exciting guest star since Janet Jackson's 'Breastgate' incident. The Bowl show had played it safe after that. Prince would change all that though. Prince would not be relying on the same old combo of fireworks, flashy technology and half-naked dancers. Nor would he be lip-synching, as Michael Jackson had in 1993, or 'pre-record' some of the vocals, as the Paul McCartney half-time show had in 2005.

Although Prince did bring with him his spectacular dancers – Australian twin sisters, Maya and Nandy McLean, aka Diamond and Pearl – his show, he declared during a warm-up concert at the Hard Rock Café in Las Vegas a few days before the Super Bowl would feature 'real music by real musicians'.

Come the night, it was that – and so much more. With the mammoth stage shaped into the 'love symbol', trimmed by purple lights and flanked by rocket bombs, searchlights crisscrossing the sky, the moment Prince was picked out by the spotlights crooning into the mike, 'Dear beloved, we are gathered here today to get through this thing called life', the 70,000-strong crowd erupted. As Prince and his band and his dancers launched into 'Let's Go Crazy', it was as if the past 30 years simply flashed by like the lights of a speeding train.

Even the fact that the Sun Life Stadium was drowned by torrential rain couldn't detract. When one of the senior members of the production team called down to Prince's dressing room half an hour before the show to talk about the rain and whether it would adversely affect Prince's plans for the show, Prince responded calmly: 'Can you make it rain harder?'

The dancers, in high heels on a stage already polished to within an inch of its life, now made so slippery it was hard to walk on without toppling, just danced even harder while

Prince threw himself around, wowing the heavens with some Hendrix-style guitar shredding. Even the local marching band, the FAMU Marching 100, were involved in 'Baby I'm a Star', all at Prince's suggestion and under his musical direction. Then a stomping 'Proud Mary', Tina Turner style, followed by 'All Along the Watchtower', for sure in the style of Hendrix, but here slowed to give it a mystical, messianic quality that suddenly took the Super Bowl show into a whole other realm. When Prince then segued his guitar solo from that into an impassioned version of the Foo Fighters' classic, 'Best of You', there was only one possible way to follow that and follow it Prince did with his final ace of the night – 'Purple Rain', the crowd inside the stadium screaming in the rain, as the Marching 100 twirled in their own purple-lit uniforms and blew their horns, Prince taking his best-known guitar solo to new, dangerously tall peaks of ecstasy as Super Bowl 41 was transformed into Purple Bowl No. 1, now recognised as probably the best Super Bowl halftime show in history. If Prince had been largely out of mainstream public view these past ten years, he was now back with a vengeance.

Most artists would have rested their case right there, but for Prince 2007 was only just getting going. In July, he shocked the British music business by releasing his new album, *Planet Earth*, as a free covermount with the *Mail on Sunday* newspaper. The album, which featured contributions from former New Power Generation members Marva King, Michael Bland and Sonny T, as well as Sheila E and former Revolution stars Wendy and Lisa, was released on NPG in the States distributed through Columbia Records, and reached No. 3. In the UK, though, it was denied an official chart position as, technically, it hadn't been sold so much as given away

– up to three million free copies, in fact.

HMV's boss, Simon Fox, described the move as 'Absolutely nuts!' Paul Quirk of the Entertainment Retailers Association was also spitting feathers. 'Prince will soon be The Artist Formerly Available in Record Stores.' Even Columbia called the giveaway 'ridiculous'. It didn't seem that way though to the three million people who bought the *Mail* that day and got the album for free. Nor did it to Prince, who was reportedly paid in the region of a million dollars for the deal, with the newspaper picking up the manufacturing and other costs. Looking back now, in fact, it makes Prince even more precognisant than ever.

With fewer people each year buying 'hard copy' forms of music – the so-called vinyl comeback still some years way and of itself only a fetish more than a real market progression – Prince had found a whole new way of getting his music heard. Later that same year Radiohead would follow Prince down a similar path with their album *In Rainbows*, whereby it was made available as a free download, with fans invited to pay as much or as little as they felt appropriate. But that was a short-lived novelty act, the album being put on general sale within weeks of the pay-what-you-want download.

One thing neither Radiohead nor anyone else was able to do that year was announce, as Prince did that summer, a non-stop 21-night residency at London's newly opened 20,000-capacity O2 arena, starting on 1 August. A few weeks before, Prince had performed a one-off gala show at the Roosevelt Hotel, in LA, for just 130 people, where tickets were priced at $3,121 a pop including dinner. For the O2 shows, though, tickets would be priced at just £31.21, including a free copy of *Planet Earth*. With each of the 21 shows sold out weeks in advance, Prince would eventually gross £11 million.

If only things could be as brilliantly worked out in his personal life. But that was one trick not even Prince was ever quite able to pull off – or not for long anyway. In 2006, it was announced that Prince's five-year marriage to Manuela Testolini was over, and that a divorce settlement had been reached. It was reported that it was Mani's decision to end the marriage and that Prince was deeply hurt. (Testolini would go on to marry Halle Berry's ex-husband, Eric Benet, in 2011 and the couple now have two daughters.)

Being Prince, though, it wasn't long before there was a new great love in his life, the singer Bria Valente, born Brenda Fuentes, who was 17 when she first met Prince, working as vocalist to Prince's brother-in-law, the keyboardist Maurice Phillips, at one of the Paisley Park studios. After that, she'd moved to LA, where she'd worked with Usher on his multi-platinum 2001 album *8701*. She had since returned to Minneapolis, providing backing vocals on *Planet Earth*. As with Mani, Bria would become a Jehovah's Witness during her relationship with Prince. She would not, however, become Mrs Prince No. 3. Prince, it seemed, had finally given up any hope of ever settling finally with just one woman.

The last few years of Prince's life followed a similar pattern. In 2010, he repeated his free giveaway feat with *Planet Earth*, with his new album, *20TEN* – the lucky recipients this time being the *Mirror* newspaper and its Scottish stable mate, the *Daily Record*. More than 2.5 million copies of the free CD were distributed with both papers in July 2010. Run alongside the giveaway were Prince-themed website features, ticket giveaways and what the *Mirror* billed as Prince's 'first British newspaper interview in more than 10 years'.

The 'exclusive interview' contained such gems as Prince saying, 'It's great to give away my music through your newspaper. God is a generous and loving being. It is written that we should act like God. There are enough opportunities.' He explained, 'There's an incredible peace in my life now and I'm trying to share it with people,' before adding, 'You know there are bad angels as well as good angels.' One can only guess at what the regular readers of the *Mirror* made of these insights, or indeed the music, but as publicity coups go this was another good one.

In fact, Prince was now giving interviews more freely than he had at any time previously in his career. One minute popping up on CNN, debating world affairs with Larry King, the next going on late-night TV in America to talk of his fear of chem-trails, his warnings about the Illuminati, his dislike of digital music, even his distaste for mobile phones.

'I personally can't stand digital music,' he told the *Guardian* in 2011. 'You're getting sound in bits. It affects a different place in your brain. When you play it back, you can't feel anything. We're analogue people, not digital.' As for phones, 'Ringtones!' he exclaimed in the same interview. 'Have you ever been in a room where there's 17 ringtones going off at once?' What about the ringtone on Prince's own phone, though? He pulled a disgusted face. 'I don't have a phone,' he fumed.

But if Prince spurned the idea that all new technology represented a leap forward – insisting until the end that he only ever record his own music on old-fashioned analogue equipment – his thirst for new experiments in sound was never quenched. In 2012, he unveiled what he now considered his ultimate backing band – an all-female trio of beautiful and enormously talented instrumentalists he named 3rdeyegirl.

It made sense. Prince had never made a secret of his preference for making music with women over men; now with 3rdeyegirl he had, he said, a band that could play better than any male musicians while looking much better doing it.

Interviewed by the writer Joel McIver, the Danish bassist, vocalist and composer Ida Nielsen, aka Bassida, aka Ida Funkhouser, revealed her background as a graduate of the Royal Danish Academy of Music. 'I played with a bunch of bands in Denmark and also with a Belgian-African band called Zap Mama. I've done a bit of international touring as well. In 2008 I released my first solo album, *Marmelade*, because I wanted to do my own music: a funk album with a lot of bass on it. I didn't care if no one wanted to listen to it, I just wanted to finally play the way I wanted. That brought me a lot of attention, so I started doing a lot of clinics and I started working with TC Electronic. I recorded a lot of videos for them, which went on YouTube around 2010 – and that was how Prince found me!

'I got a call from his manager, but I thought it was a joke. She invited me over to Paisley Park for a jam and I said "Sure!" and she told me she'd call me back. But I didn't hear anything for two weeks, so I thought that was it . . . then I finally got the call and went to Minneapolis – and three months later I was on tour with Prince.'

She recalled how 'super sweet' Prince was. 'He asked me which kind of basses I had and stuff like that, to help me relax and get into nerd mode. After a few minutes it was cool and we started jamming. Prince asked me if I could go on tour with him, so I learned a whole bunch of songs. There was a lot of stuff to remember, because he likes to change things up and not always stick to what's on the set list, so I had a lot of different songs to learn in a short time, that was the hardest part of it. It wasn't like a normal gig where you have 30 songs: I had to learn 300 songs. That took a lot of time.'

In the same interview, the drummer Hannah Welton-Ford, 22 years old and from Louisville, Kentucky, revealed how she first met Prince. 'I got a random email in 2012 from this person who said that she managed a very well-known musician. She was wondering if I would be interested in auditioning for an upcoming project that she had. She couldn't give me any more details – but she wanted to know if I could keep a secret!'

A few days later she was at church, 'working with a couple of kids in the team ministry', when she got another email. 'I checked it, and she'd written back and said "OK great! I work for Prince. He's seen some of your videos on YouTube, and would love it if you were interested in auditioning for his upcoming project" – and I freaked out . . .'

Invited to Paisley Park, she thought perhaps she was dreaming, she said. 'It's beautiful, first of all – like a fairytale wonderland. To this day, every time I go in there I feel like I see something new that I've never seen before. It's incredible to be surrounded by such success on a daily basis. But when I first got there I didn't know what to expect. Well, you hear a lot about Prince on the outside about how he's very mysterious.

'I was taken back into one of his studio rooms and was told to fix the drum set however I liked it, so I was by myself doing that and he just walked in. He shook my hand and said, "Hi, I'm Prince. It's great to meet you, thank you for coming" and the very first question he asked me was "Do you play ping pong?" And from that moment it was very comfortable: there were no nervous, awkward moments. I felt right at home immediately.

'Sometimes people don't believe us when we say we're not sure where we're going to be tomorrow, as far as touring and stuff goes,' Hannah went on. 'When we did all the hit-and-run gigs over there in the UK [in 2014], we literally did not know where we were going. We found out about those gigs online, like everyone else did! It blows people away, but it keeps things interesting at our end because no one gig is ever the same as another. Our lives are like that too: sporadic and spontaneous. This time tomorrow we could be on the other side of the world. It's a big adventure.'

And it wasn't over yet.

11

Sometimes It Snows in April

When Prince's adventures finally came to an end in the early hours of the morning, on 21 April 2016, it shocked the whole world. Over his 35-year career we had grown accustomed to being constantly surprised with his latest move, good or bad, safe or sexy, but this was something so ghastly, so unexpected, no one could have seen it coming.

Officers had been called to Paisley Park at 9.43 a.m. and found 'an unresponsive male in an elevator'. At 10.07 a.m. Prince was pronounced dead. There were reportedly no signs of foul play. 'There are no further details as to the cause of death at this time,' Carver County sheriff's office said in a statement. 'It is with profound sadness that I am confirming that the legendary, iconic performer, Prince Rogers Nelson, has died,' Anna Meacham, his publicist, said. Police had 'no reason to believe' he killed himself, it was also reported, as though that eased the agony for his fans, and there were 'no obvious signs of trauma' on his body.

The words just seemed too small to try and somehow explain what had just happened. Too blurry and somehow inappropriate, too non-specific to offer any real insight. The big questions everyone was asking now were: how and why? Prince was only 57, a well-known teetotaller and vegan who had spent his life warning against the evils of drugs. A guy who could still dance around the stage like a man half his age. How could someone like that just one day . . . die?

Within days conspiracy theories were all over the internet. Prince had been murdered by the Illuminati – for speaking out about chem-trails, as payback for his victory over Warner's, because Prince was about to reveal everything he knew about the underworld of secret powerbrokers that really ruled the world. That was why his body had been secretly cremated in an intimate ceremony at a nondescript funeral home in Minneapolis shortly after an autopsy was completed the day after his death. According to reports, only Prince's sister, Tyka Nelson, and another unnamed family member were allowed to spend a few minutes saying goodbye during a visit to the First Memorial Waterston Chapel before the musician was cremated.

The latter part about Prince's cremation was true enough, but as for the rest of this nonsense, what were Prince's fans to believe? Slowly, though, over the coming weeks, a picture began to emerge. Not of a god residing on a purple cloud but of a vulnerable man, whose failing health he was now apparently self-medicating to help alleviate. Some sources quoted in major news outlets claimed Prince had begun taking ultra-strong opiates to relieve chronic pain in his hips. Doctors had advised him he needed double-hip replacement surgery but that Prince refused it on the grounds of his religious beliefs, as Jehovah's Witnesses eschew blood transfusions in favour of prayers. While another, more disturbing source claimed that Prince had been buying controlled-substance painkillers for over 30 years.

'The hip and ankle issues were a problem for him for so long,' *Entertainment Tonight*'s Kevin Frazier told CBS News in the States, saying Prince also suffered chronic pain in his ankles as well as his hips. 'For a man who loved to move and dance so much, it really bothered him,' Frazier said. It was later reported that Prince had, in fact, gone ahead and had a private operation on his hips as far back as 2010. One of the reasons he'd carried a cane with him ever since – usually assumed to be an affectation rather than a medical necessity. 'Walking around with a cane was not just to look supercool,' Prince's longtime hairstylist Kim Berry had been quoted as saying recently.

To add to his growing list of ailments in later years, Prince confessed, he now suffered from chronic insomnia. 'I always wanted to be really famous,' he reflected sadly. 'But now, just like Elvis, I find myself a prisoner of my fame.'

Was all of this true? New and more ghastly stories seemed to be emerging every day. The *National Enquirer*, America's most notorious supermarket tabloid, announced on its front page just three weeks later that Prince had died of 'full-blown AIDS'. The paper quoted an unnamed source who claimed, it said, that 'Prince was diagnosed with "full-blown AIDS"' six months before. The source also revealed to the *Enquirer*, it claimed, that Prince had 'refused all medical treatments, believing he could be cured by prayer!' The paper included the astonishing claim that Prince's family were insisting 'the medical examiner's toxicology report be "heavily censored" to respect Prince's privacy', then concluded with its unnamed source claiming, 'Doctors told Prince his blood count was unusually low and that his body temperature had dropped dangerously below the normal 98.6 degrees to 94 degrees. He was totally iron-deficient, very weak and often disoriented. He rarely ate and when he did, it all came right back up.'

It seemed the mystery that always surrounded his life would only deepen with his death. The only thing that seemed to be certain was that Prince, for the final years of his life at least, had been guarding a secret. One he would eventually take with him to his grave. A study of the facts produces a disturbing portrait of a man whose woeful death belied his avowed mission always to celebrate life, through music, through sex, through God.

The first signs of something not being as it was supposed to seem from the outside occurred in the early 2000s, when his half-brother, Duane, reportedly informed his lawyer that Prince was addicted to cocaine and Percocet – the latter a ferociously strong painkiller often prescribed by doctors to someone who has recently undergone major surgery.

The first the world got wind of anything being really wrong with Prince, though, came when his private plane was forced to make an emergency landing on 15 April, as Prince and his entourage flew home from a concert in Atlanta, the plane descending 45,000 feet in just 17 minutes after an 'unresponsive male' was reported on board, with the fire department and paramedics alerted of the incoming patient.

At the time, Prince's official management sources put out a press release explaining that Prince simply had a bad case of flu. It has since emerged, however, that an unconscious Prince was carried off the plane by his bodyguard, straight into a limo which sped to nearby Moline hospital, where the Emergency Medical Services team hurriedly administered a 'save shot' – medical slang for an injection of the anti-overdose medication Narcan, given to victims of drug overdoses in life-threatening conditions. The doctors at the hospital were so concerned they insisted that Prince stay in for the next 24 hours. But

Prince shrugged off the suggestion, ordering his team to take him back to his plane just three hours later, and get him home again.

The story was widely reported around the world but any suspicions that this was anything more than the 'severe flu' were quickly allayed when Prince was seen bicycling around the Paisley Park compound the next day. That night he also held an impromptu concert at Paisley Park, showing off a new purple piano and assuring the crowd of fan club members, family and friends they should 'Wait a few days before you waste any prayers.'

Two nights before his death Prince was seen attending a performance by the jazz singer Lizz Wright at a local club called the Dakota. The following day though, according to a report in *Rolling Stone*, Prince met with Michael Schulenberg, a family-medicine doctor, who issued an 'unidentified pre-scription, his second in a few weeks from the same doctor. Later that day, Prince was photographed outside a local Wal-greens [pharmacy].' It was later that night, *Rolling Stone* went on to report, that 'Someone in Prince's camp reached out to Howard Kornfeld, a Mill Valley, California, doctor who runs an outpatient clinic that specializes in treating addictions.'

According to the report, Kornfeld's son Andrew took an overnight flight to Minneapolis, but by the time he arrived at Paisley Park the following morning Prince was dead. His body had been found slumped in one of the building's eleva-tors. Reports later suggested that police on the scene recovered paraphernalia and paperwork to indicate that Prince had been taking doses of Percocet, along with other possible sub-stances. The DEA later let it be known that they would be questioning anyone they suspected of helping supply Prince with painkillers.

Most damning of all was a story run in the online edition of the *Mail*, 48 hours after Prince's death, purporting to be an interview with Prince's main drug dealer, who wished to be identified only as Doctor D. Whoever this was, he claimed that Prince usually paid him, sometimes $40,000 a time, in exchange for six-month medical supplies of Dilaudid pills and Fentanyl patches – both in the same category at Percocet as grade-A super-strength opioid painkillers

According to Doctor D, Prince was 'majorly addicted' and first bought drugs from him as far back as 1984, remaining in touch until around 2008. The self-confessed drug dealer, who was a familiar face to many celebrities and musicians over those years, claimed it began because Prince suffered such debilitating stage fright he had come to use the drugs as a crutch to help him perform.

'I first met Prince in 1984 while he was filming the movie *Purple Rain*,' he told the *Mail*. 'I didn't hook him on drugs, he was already a really heavy user. In the beginning he would buy speed as well as Dilaudid. He would use that as a counter-balance to get back up again from taking opiates. That lasted for a couple of years then he would just buy Dilaudid, which is a heroin-based opiate.'

Doctor D insisted he'd never known Prince to take street heroin, 'as that would leave you out of it for days whereas Dilaudid gives you an energy buzz as well as making you feel relaxed, so he preferred it'. He added a horribly plausible detail. Prince craved the drugs, he said, 'because he was so nervous. He could be nervous in a room with just five people in it. He was scared to go out in public, he was scared to talk to people, and didn't like to go on stage . . .'

At the time of going to press, results from the autopsy had only just been released, confirming what many feared: that Prince had died of an accidental overdose of Fentanyl – the powerful synthetic opiate said to be much more potent than morphine, often used to alleviate the suffering of cancer patients.

Prophetically, Cyril Wecht, a forensic pathologist uncon-nected to the case, when interviewed by NBC TV's *Today* show, said, 'I would give overwhelming odds that, tragically, this is a drug death. When you rule out foul play, when there is no history of any kind of significant disease, when you rule out any kind of intervention, anything of an environmental nature, you come down to an autopsy that is essentially nega-tive and that probably means drugs.'

According to Doctor D, Prince's dependence on the drugs he was supplying grew to the extent where he was taking double or triple the recommended medial dose. This included the wearing of Fentanyl patches, which police and paramedics were reported to have found on Prince's dead body. 'They come in boxes of five and I would sell Prince 20 boxes at a time.'

Because Prince was such a private, even secretive person, it's not difficult to understand how this sort of behaviour might have gone on for years without those close to him suspecting anything. The fact that he always made such a big deal over what food he ate, what beverages he let pass his lips – no alco-hol, not even any tea or coffee – again, it's easy to see why no one would have looked twice at the idea that he might secret-ly be taking drugs. Doctor D recalled how, once, Prince was 'eating a salad and a skinless chicken breast with no dressing and I commented about how healthy he was. He turned to me and said, "If I didn't watch my food I probably wouldn't last that long." I think it was his way of counteracting all the drugs he was taking.'

Could all this be true? Certainly the police were investigating such claims very seriously. A police source told the *Mirror*: 'We understand Prince suffered chronic pain after developing a hip problem. Naturally he took painkillers to ease his troubles but police are looking into if he was prescribed too many. We have seen in the case of [Michael] Jackson how people can acquire large quantities of drugs when really they should be monitored.' How awfully ironic, if it turned out to be true that the same self-administered pain pills killed both Prince and his one-time rival, Michael Jackson?

In another sad irony, the dealer recalled how Prince would often talk to him about God during their sporadic meetings, even going so far as to invite him to Jehovah's Witness Bible study groups. 'He often used to preach about God to me. Maybe it was a form of guilt . . . He'd say, "You know there's only one God and we're all here for a reason, to serve God." And he'd say, "We have to be good people, it's important that we try to be good people." He had a thing about being a good person.'

Yes, he did. And we should hold on to that knowledge now we start to hear about those sides of Prince he was too ashamed to ever let the world see while he was alive. A philanderer on the scale of Casanova, a musical genius as close to God as Miles Davis or Jimi Hendrix, Prince was also a conduit for acceptance and understanding for races and creeds from all corners of the world, no matter what their sexuality, age, background or talents. It was all there in his multi-coloured, multicultural music, all roads leading to the same destination.

That was certainly the larger message being given out in the days that followed his death. A week after he died, Prince had no fewer than five albums in the US Top 10, including the No. 1 and No. 2 spots with *The Very Best of Prince* and *Purple Rain*, respectively. Prince's overall catalogue of albums sold 256,000 copies that week, reported *Billboard*, an increase of 5,298 per cent compared to the previous week's estimated sales of around 5,000. The same week, in Britain, Prince held all five of the Top 5 positions in the albums chart, plus four in the Top 5 of the singles chart, with 'Purple Rain' at No. 1, 'When Doves Cry' at No. 2, 'Kiss' at No. 4 and '1999' in fifth position.

The day after his death, thousands of fans continued to arrive at his home to pay their respects. Many left purple flowers, while others wrote messages of love on huge posters tied to the fence. Thousands more also gathered at the First Avenue club in Minneapolis, where Prince recorded the film version of *Purple Rain*, while others held vigils across the US and the rest of the world. Coming out to address the mourners outside Paisley Park, his brother-in-law, Maurice Phillips, said Prince had appeared 'pale' and 'weak' before his death after he stayed awake for six days. He reportedly told the fans: 'He worked 154 hours straight. I was with him just last weekend. He was a good brother-in-law.' Maurice's wife, Prince's sister, Tyka Nelson, also came outside to tell the crowd: 'He loved all of you. Thank you for loving him back.'

In New York, the filmmaker Spike Lee threw a street party in honour of Prince for around 1,000 people at his Brooklyn headquarters. The crowd danced and sang along to 'Little Red Corvette', 'I Wanna Be Your Lover' and 'If I Was Your Girlfriend'. Dressed in a purple T-shirt, Lee also led the crowd through an encore of 'Purple Rain'. Many other stars paid tribute, Mike Tyson tweeting a weird picture of himself with his face transposed with Prince's. Mariah Carey stopped her show in Paris and gave tribute.

Movingly, Britain's Rita Ora, who had worked with Prince on her massive 2015 hit 'Ain't About 2 Stop', said, 'This is coming from a place I never knew existed in my heart. You were so special to me, your presence, the music we created, the dance-offs we used to have and the laughter we shared.' She went on: 'The funk oozing out of you was uncontrollable. I'm not quite sure what to do with myself but I will miss you for ever and always, my dear kind friend.'

Paloma Faith wrote on Twitter: 'The greatest living musician is now no longer with us and I'm distraught. It was a pleasure to share a stage with him. Prince, fly with the doves.'

More poignantly, Mayte Garcia, who had been mother to Prince's only child, wept as she told reporters, 'I can't even think of the words of what I'm feeling. This man was my everything. We had a family. I am beyond deeply saddened and devastated.' She sobbed as she added, 'I loved him then, I love him now and will love him eternally. He's with our son now.' Sheila E tweeted: 'My heart is broken. There are no words. I love you!'

We all did.

Invited to reflect, briefly, in 2004, on the vicissitudes of getting older, of peering forward towards that endless night that awaits us all, Prince pursed his lips into that inscrutable secret smile that seemed to say I-know-something-you-don't. Then said, simply, 'I don't look at time that way, and I don't believe in age. When you wake up, each day looks the same, so each day should be a new beginning. I don't have an expiration date.'

And Prince really doesn't. You can grab your phone and listen to one of his immortal tunes right now. Or turn to a computer and pull up a million and one of his million-to-one performances.

Or as he once sang it so sweetly on that song the whole world now knows, 'I only wanted to see you bathing in the purple rain . . .'

Catch U there.

Notes and Sources

Grateful acknowledgement and thanks to the following writers, publications, broadcasts and blogs for inspiration, background, quotes, opinions right and wrong, and most of all a sense of place and time. All of us who wrote about Prince at different points of his story only ever got most of it right some of the time. But that's one of the many things that drew us to write about him. You never quite knew the beginning, the middle or the end of any part of it. Only where the story looked right then from where we stood. Looking back, it's amazing how much we all got wrong. And even more amazing how some of us were so right.

Those that got it right in the newspapers and magazines were top-of-the-heap cats like Phil Sutcliffe, Jeff Lorez, Per Nilsen, Ronin Ro, Chris Salewicz, Andy Schwartz, and Anthony DeCurtis in heavyweight rock'n'roll journals like *Rolling Stone*, *Mojo*, *Q*, *NME*, *The Word*, *Melody Maker* and *Billboard*.

But there were also precious pieces to the Prince story that only got picked up on the hoof by people who were covering the story here and there. In places as big and less big but just as important as the *New York Times*, the *LA Times*, *The Guardian*, *The London Times*, *The Mail*, *The Mirror*, *New York News*, *People*, *Times Herald-Record*, *Vibe*, *Out*, *New York Rocker*, *The*

Face, Smash Hits, Star Tribune, Uptown, Creem, Star News, the *Beautiful Nights Blog* and *www.biography.com.*

Then there were the books, amazing and thoroughly recommended further reading:

21 Nights, Prince, Simon & Schuster, 2008

Glow: The Autobiography of Rick James, Rick James, Atria, 2014

Let's Go Crazy, Prince and the Making of Purple Rain, Alan Light, Atria, 2014

Miles: The Autobiography, Miles Davis, Picador, 1990

Prince, Matt Thorne, Faber & Faber, 2013

Prince: Chaos, Disorder and Revolution, Jason Draper, Backbeat 2011

Prince: Inside The Music and the Masks, Ronin Ro, Aurum, 2012

The Beat of My Own Drum, Sheila E, Atria, 2014

And then those things that came along only once but when rediscovered offered a certain wow factor too: the 2011 BBC4 TV doc, *Purple Reign*. Alicia Keys 2004 Rock and Roll Hall of Fame induction speech. Joel McIver's in-depth interviews with the girls of 3rdeyegirl. All the crazy clips now collected on *YouTube* from various TV appearances through the years: Prince on *MTV, CNN, Oprah Winfrey*, the *Superbowl*, Prince killing twice over 20 years on *Arsenio Hall*. . . the list is almost endless.

Indeed, just as it did for Jimi Hendrix, Elvis Presley, John Lennon, Bob Marley and others, the story of Prince will not end with his death. The afterlife for Prince has already begun.

Index